Oddballs

The Social Maverick and the Dynamics of Individuality

Bernard G. Suran

Nelson-Hall *nh* Chicago

Librabry of Congress Cataloging in Publication Data

Suran, Bernard G.
    Oddballs.

    Includes bibliographical references and index.
    1. Individuality. 2. Eccentricity and eccentrics.
I. Title.
BF697.S93   155.2'32   77-16660
ISBN 0-88229-366-4 (cloth)
ISBN 0-88229-557-8 (paper)

Manufactured in the United States of America.

10   9   8   7   6   5   4   3   2   1

The fly sat upon
   the axle-tree of the chariot wheel
     and said,
       "what a dust do I raise."

Francis Bacon, *Of Vain Glory*

Demens judicio vulgi,
Sanus fortasse tuo.

Mad in the judgment of the mob,
Sane perhaps in your own.

Horace, *Satires*, Book I, 6

The truly mature individual may at times forsake adjustment and conformity for the less certain and more painful, but ultimately more rewarding and constructive experience of attempting to alter or influence his world in a creative fashion.

Group for the Advancement of Psychiatry, *Psychopathological Disorders of Childhood*

New York: GAP, 1966, p. 187.

Contents

Acknowledgments

ALTHOUGH THE THEME of this book celebrates the individualizing self, the author recognizes all too well that selves become individualized only through clarifying interaction with other individualizing selves. A note of appreciation is in order to the many individuals who have helped the author clarify the material included in the manuscript: to Jerome L. Schulman, M.D., for his constant support and encouragement as well as his consummate willingness always to be himself, even when I didn't want him to be; to Stanley Lipkin, Ph.D., for his assistance in identifying some very personal roots of individuation; to the Drs. Sheridan and the Drs. Wolfe, who have put up with some fairly strange shenanigans; most especially, to Mary Elizabeth Suran, Ph.D., who somehow has made it all better. Special thanks also to Ms. Roberta Woods, Ms. Carolyn Schroeder, and especially Ms. Virginia Gilman for assistance in the preparation of the manuscript.

1

An Introduction to the Oddball

WHY WOULD ANYBODY want to write a book about oddballs? Unquestionably, this is a fair question, and if the reader is to continue with this little volume, he or she should have a clear idea of its purpose. My developing interest in oddballitry was catalyzed some years ago while I was viewing an old Frank Sinatra movie in which Sinatra played a tough-talking, hard-nosed detective named Tony Rome. It was not one of Sinatra's more stellar roles, but some place near the middle of the movie, Sinatra spat out a line that cut me to the quick. Sinatra-as-Rome was involved in a heated conversation with a smooth-talking psychiatrist, whose name I never knew or can't recall. At the height of their exchange, Sinatra-as-Rome bellowed out his contempt for psychiatry in a one-liner that started my insides churning. "I know what psychiatry is," said Sinatra-as-Rome. "Psychiatry is a way of teaching healthy people to adjust to a sick world."

As a young, dedicated psychotherapist, I was disturbed by the truth of this observation. It was already becoming clear to me that many of the problems encountered in people who sought psychotherapy were not problems with themselves but problems encountered with the world in which they lived. There were, of course, new movements within the profession. Radical psychotherapy, with all of its sundry manifestations, was just coming into vogue. "Therapy means change" became the touchstone of a whole new spate of therapeutic literature, and the radical psychotherapists were encouraging their patients to confront the worlds in which they lived rather than turning inward on themselves. For therapists who were trained in the sixties, an era of social upheaval and revolution, it became expedient to work out a point of view that would consider both the ills of society as well as the ills of the individual patient.

In my own practice, I gradually began to settle on a philosophy of treatment and social change that enabled me to function as a psychotherapist. I began to see myself as an agent of personal change. My interests and my investment would be with the individual client. I would not help people "adjust." Rather, I would help them realize themselves. Perhaps the difference was merely one of semantics, but I found myself not giving a damn about what the world was like. The important issue was the way in which the world was experienced by my client. I was not training people how to adjust to the world. I was helping them create a world of their own making, at least the world that they directly experienced. Psychotherapy became for me a vehicle by which clients could explore their sense of who they were or wished to become.

This, of course, is not an original point of view, and when one makes an investment in people as people, in individuals as individuals, strange things begin to happen. One's tolerance for "craziness" increases significantly. I began to realize that, in order to be healthy, everybody needs to be a little bit crazy. In order to be healthy, a person needs to "not give a damn about what the world is like." In order to explore oneself as an individual, one must be able to set aside the customs and conventions of society. As an advocate for the individual person, I became increasingly aware that there was no one correct world or one correct way to be within the world.

In time, I began to see that the function of the psychotherapist was neither to support nor to deny the social order, whatever its strengths or weaknesses; rather, the function of the psychotherapist is to advocate and celebrate the individualizing self. *Oddballs*, then, is intended to be exactly such a celebration, and it seeks both to investigate as well as pay tribute to certain individuals who have learned to do their own thing, irrespective of the social implications.

In many ways, *Oddballs* represents my own ax-grinding with regard to the therapeutic professionals who continue to show overwhelming concern for social conventions at the expense of the individualizing self. It seems to me, rightly or wrongly, that psychotherapy is one of the last bastions for the individual *qua* individual. A therapist may well wear many hats and function in a variety of ways for a particular client, but I cannot help but believe that psychotherapy is for the individual as an individual. When a therapist becomes a moralist, an arbiter of social values and societal expectations, then that unique, idiosyncratic side of the individual self will inevitably be insufficiently explored and supported. The temptation to help someone "adjust to the world" is stronger than sanity itself, whatever that means. As I read the viewpoints of my fellows, it is painfully clear that the conscience of the psychotherapist is terribly conservative and betrays an overwhelming need for social approval. Whatever became of radical psychotherapy? Is psychotherapy a way of helping people gain the approval of the world, or is it a means of enabling people to approve of themselves?

These are a few of the inner rumblings that have brought me to *Oddballs*, but I would be false to myself if I were to disguise this work as a totally professional concern. I have always liked "weird" people, whether they were crazy or not. I can recall that, early in my youth, I was fascinated at the sight of one of the characters who peopled the neighborhood in which I was raised. The strange little lady who lived alone and kept a houseful of cats, and never cut her grass or trimmed her hedge, so that her house was swallowed by vines. How we always wondered what went on inside that mysterious house! And how I wondered what went on inside that mysterious lady!

I'm sure that all of us grew up in some way wondering about the screwballs who peopled our respective neighborhoods. When I finally arrived in graduate school, I was so disappointed to find out that these mysterious screwballs of my youth were actually psychotics and neurotics and psychopaths and social deviants and so on. Somewhere down deep I guess I believed that such people were just different, no more and no less—just different. Quite frankly, I would rather believe in oddballs than in the Diagnostic and Statistical Manual of the American Psychiatric Association, which is known to produce and discard diagnoses at a rate rapidly approaching the speed of light.

The Diagnostic Manual of the APA, as well as most textbooks on abnormal psychology, provides yet another reason to grieve about the fate of the individualizing self in the contemporary world. Most of the people who write books and ply their trade in the mental health professions are the products of middle-class backgrounds. By and large, they cannot help but be extremely conventional folk who look at life from the wide end of the funnel, which means that the scene is very narrow at the other end. The patient never gets a break. A patient can't be somebody who is just a little offbeat or struggling with the problems of living or searching for some sense of meaning about himself or at odds with the sickness of the world or whatever would make him seem like a genuine individual human being. Oh, no! The patient is "classifiable" according to the middle-class mental health mythology. If the patient isn't labeled as having some identifiable form of insanity, then the whole profession is in trouble. The inevitable result is that anybody who doesn't behave or believe according to the conventional standards is necessarily viewed by the mental health establishment as certifiable funny-farm material. A quick review of the Diagnostic Manual will reveal that there are almost a thousand ways by which we can label someone "crazy," ranging from the more harmless "passive-aggressive personality, passive type" to the more awesome "manic-depressive psychosis, manic state."

I would be the first to admit that some people are crazier than others, but it is also my firm belief that most patients and clients are not as crazy as the mental health professionals give them credit for being. I am happy to say that I have had the privilege of treating some very squirrelly people in my professional life, people who would be labeled "chronic schizophrenic" and such by diagnosticians. To a large extent, I have found the patients to be not significantly different in nature than many of the professionals who do the diagnosing. Less pompous, perhaps. Much more into their own thing, perhaps. More individualized, perhaps. Not fitting into conventional society, perhaps. Oddballs, definitely.

Which brings me back to the point of this book, namely that there is no line between genius and insanity. Rather, there are only various degrees of individuation. Nobody is crazy. Some people are a lot more like a lot of other people. Some people are a little more different. And all of us are faced with the issue of what it means to be ourselves, simply and purely our individual selves, in a world that wants everyone to be alike. There can be no doubt that society places a premium on conformity and conventionality. The most striking example of this fact is contemporary Russia, which judges its political dissidents to be insane and sends them to asylums for the mentally incompetent. Under guard. And yet, Russia is only an extreme example of the way in which social groups protect themselves and their standards from the unpredictable vicissitudes of true individuals. All societies and social groups have reason to fear the unusual individual, the person who thinks differently or whose behavior is at odds with that of his contemporaries.

Which brings us to a definition of the oddball. *Webster's Unabridged* (3rd edition) recognizes the oddball as "one whose behavior is eccentric or otherwise peculiar." *Webster's New World Dictionary* tells us that an oddball is "an eccentric, unconventional, or nonconforming person." The *American Heritage Dictionary of the English Language* goes a step further and defines an oddball as "a person marked by eccentric behavior or way of thinking." I guess a more complete definition would designate the oddball as "someone who departs from, or fails to conform to, the real or imagined conventions of appearance, behavior, ideas, or what-have-you that tend to reflect the established patterns of a particular social group." More succinctly, an oddball is simply a person who has become sufficiently individualized so that he or she is distinguishable from most members of the social group. Quite typically, oddballs are judged to be crazy by their peers, although from another vantage, they may well be the bastions of sanity in a world gone mad.

It is my contention that even though society fears the unusual person, it is, nonetheless, the oddball who is the source of social development and cultural enrichment in the world. In short, it is the crazy people who make the world go. *Oddballs* is an attempt to explore this hypothesis. This is not a conventional psychological study, and true to this spirit, it violates most canons of scientific investigation. The tone varies from deadly serious to mildly zany to genuinely profane, but, through it all, I will maintain the point of view that it is better to be crazy than to be like everybody else. In order to be healthy, everybody needs to be at least a little bit different; in *Oddballs* we will examine several individuals who have achieved the heights of difference.

In a more serious, philosophical sense, this study attempts to investigate the inborn tension that I believe exists between the individual and the social group that forms and informs the individual self. An inescapable fact of human experience and science is that individual human persons are formed and informed by the societies in which they live. But, oh the paradox! At the same time, social groups themselves are the very creation of the individuals that such societies are forming and informing. This intriguing mutuality and inter-relatedness between the human as an individual and human society as a social group is an issue of central concern and maximum import to the various philosophies and sciences, and it is the undercurrent and foundational theme of this investigation. Societies are true to themselves to the extent that they are able to entice the various members to form themselves in the image of the social context; to be "socialized" is to conform to the laws, conventions, and expectations that govern a particular society. In order to be "individualized," is it necessary to discard the conventions of a given society? *Oddballs* will argue in the affirmative—that in order to come to some degree of individual well-being, it is absolutely essential to distinguish oneself from the social mass. Oddballs are, by definition, social mavericks, and the point of view here advanced maintains that there is something very healthy about being a social maverick. The madness that comes from within is just as honorable or as dishonorable as the madness that exists within the world.

I should go a step further. Oddballitry, the art of being an individual, is good not only for the individual practitioner, but also for society. There is much to be learned from the study of oddballs. Many of the most significant human advances have been brought to fruition by genuine weirdoes. The influence of the oddball on human history and progress is so significant that without them we might yet be living in the caves or swinging from tree to tree. Can you imagine the fear and shock that must have gripped the first society when the original free blithe spirit brought a torch into the cave and suggested that everyone dine that night on roast mastodon? And yet, where would we be if we had not harnessed fire itself! As we shall see, oddballs are good for the world.

In order to deal with the deeper meanings and the lessons of the oddball, we must first come to grips with the issues of convention and conformity. These determine whether oddballs are genuine or not. When an oddball becomes sufficiently conforming and conventional, even to a group of odder-balls, he may well have forsaken real, dynamic oddballitry for the straight path of conforming conventionality. Oddballs are defined by their clear departure from a set of conventions, and they are broken by any growing allegiance to a new set of conventions. That is not to say that oddballs do not have patterns and conventions of their own. This is precisely the point: such patterns and conventions are truly *their own* and not merely those of the social group. This book, therefore, is as much an investigation of conventions and conformity as it is a study of oddballs.

What do we mean by conventions and conformity? Habits. Manners. Customs. Formulas. Standards. Practices. Formalities. Bylaws. Proprieties. Routines. Folkways, usages, and mores. Expectations. Regulations. Statutes. Norms. Beliefs. Codes. Creeds. Commandments. Traditions. Morals. Ethics. Laws. The approved and accepted and agreed-upon and orthodox ways of doing and being, and all the various kinds of social structures and strictures to which flesh is heir. The usual, the normal, the very heartbeat and *raison d'etre* of the social group. This is the feel, the intellectual and emotional grip, of convention. A convention is the glue of the social group, that which renders the members of the group agreeable and/or alike. Convention is the stuff of society.

The highly individualized person is exactly what convention is not. The oddball. Queer. Crackpot. Fluke. Crank. Geek. Freak. Wack. Screwball. Fish out of water. One in a million. Eccentric. Weird. Unheard of. Prodigy. Unparall-

eled. Outlandish. Exotic. Offbeat. Extraordinary. Noteworthy. Bizarre. Grotesque. *Sui generis*. Neither fish nor
fowl. Alien. Strange. Outcast. A character. A card. Pariah. A
curiosity. Unfashionable. Irregular. Unconventional and un-
conforming. Abnormal. An anomaly. Uncommon. Rare. Exceptional. Singular. Aberrant. Individual. The few-and-far-
betweens by which one distinguishes oneself from the
aspects of the many. The very stuff by which the individual is
truly individualized. This is the feel, the intellectual and
emotional grip, of individuality.

There are obviously a wide variety of expressive terms
and ideas that could apply to the realities I am here attempting to describe and approximate. I have chosen, however, to
work within the framework of oddballs and oddballitry
because I feel these terms best capture and epitomize the
spirit and the focus of this study. Crackpots and crack-
pottery were a tempting designation, but my handy desk dictionary defined the crackpot as "an extreme fanatic." It is my
belief that fanaticism is only one of the possible manifestations of individualism. The term *oddball* tends to be less
offensive to the conventionally inclined and seems more
harmless than many other possible terms that might help
unravel the underlying realities. At the same time, I am
convinced that *oddball* is much closer to a sensible reality
than *psychotic* or *genius,* which are common ways of desig-
nating people who are different; *oddball* simply connotes the
feeling of someone sticking out like a sore thumb, namely the
highly unique individual who coexists with the more
commonplace. There are undoubtedly a number of people
who will be offended by the designation of certain characters
in this study as oddballs. Let them, then, take umbrage. I do
not believe that a study of this kind can be done without upsetting a few conventional apple carts. All of the characters in
this study share to some degree an irreverence for common
idols and a sense of iconoclasm that causes them to step
beyond the rudiments of conventional experience in order to

achieve a unique posture and a solitary vision. As Thoreau, all of the other characters studied herein are able to say, "I can only sense progress when I am swimming against the stream."

What I am trying to say, perhaps with unnecessary circularity, is that a human is a blend of both the common and unique, but the unique is much more difficult to understand and appreciate than the common. *Oddballs* is not merely an offbeat worship of the weird or a celebration of zaniness. I come to this study with a desire to make sense of the sources of individuation within the human person as well as a desire to understand the legitimate workings of social conventions. Oddballitry runs as many risks as does idolatry and the worship of common idols; offbeat gods are neither better nor worse that the conventional gods. When all is said and done, what does it mean to be fully human? Does it mean being highly socialized? Or does it mean being highly individualized? Is it possible to be both? Are these the polar extremities of the human spectrum? Are some conventions and social groups more conducive to individuality than others? Are some expressions of individuality more supportive of the social group than others? Are there better and worse solutions to the inevitable and ongoing conflict between individuals and social groups? These are some of the questions that have prodded my consciousness throughout this investigation.

Oddballs, then, seeks to illumine the complex interactions between the normative influence of the social group and the inherent drive to be oneself, between the generalized acceptance of the conventional wisdom and the curious goads and challenges of the individual seeker-of-truth, between the pull of the many and the thrust of the one. Obviously, some people feel the call to selfhood more strongly than others, and I have attempted to seek out a variety of individuals who in their own unique way demonstrate their respective drives toward individuality. Why, for example, did Sigmund Freud frame his revolutionary theory of human behavior in a sexual framework and language that he knew would be offensive to his colleagues? Why did Diogenes, the ancient Greek philosopher, walk the streets of Athens stark naked except for the proverbial barrel? Why did the audience at the Paris Opera House stage a full-scale riot and revolt at Igor Stravinsky's introduction of a new musical composition, the *Rite of Spring*? Why did James Joyce cast his last novel, *Finnegans Wake*, in a strange, new, hybrid language that could not be understood by anyone except himself? Why did Ezekiel the Prophet literally eat his own book of prophecy? Why did Charles Darwin risk the stigma of heresy by publishing his highly offbeat view that man and apes were descended from a common ancestor? Why did Jerry Rubin answer his subpoena by the House UnAmerican Activities Committee by appearing before HUAC dressed in the garb of an American Revolutionary soldier and passing out parchment copies of the Declaration of Independence? Oddballs all? Or bearers of a special wisdom and teachers of a unique truth?

The chapters which follow are loosely organized into sections. Part I deals with oddball ideas about man's origins; it examines three outstanding oddballs: Erich von Daniken, Charles Darwin, and Moses. Part II deals with oddball behavior and reviews Diogenes of Sinope, the prophet Ezekiel, and Jerry Rubin. Part III studies three oddballs in the arts: Igor Stravinsky, James Joyce, and Lenny Bruce. Part IV investigates several representative oddballs in the social sciences, including Orson Fowler and the science of phrenology, Sigmund Freud and the science of psychoanalysis, and B. F. Skinner and the science of behavioral psychology. A concluding chapter will attempt to pull together this investigation and to work toward the establishment of a coherent theory of individuality.

Part One

Oddball Ideas and the Theory of Man's Origins

2 Erich von Daniken

The Martians Have Come, The Martians Have Gone

HOW DOES ONE decide who is a genuine oddball, and which oddballs should be selected for a particular collection? It should be reiterated that oddballitry is a very inexact science, at least in the hands of this practitioner, and the selection of oddballs encountered herein is intended to be neither exhaustive nor exclusive. The choice of oddballs in this study is purely dependent on the ability of the individual selected to illustrate certain themes. It is not necessarily a matter of seeking out the oddestballs, and there are undoubtedly odderballs living in your own neighborhood. I trust that no one will be offended by exclusion.

Obviously, there are no preordained, conventional ways to structure a study of this nature, and one would hope to have sufficient freedom to proceed according to the movements of the spirit. I would like to begin, however, with an area of central concern and considerable importance to both professional and layman alike, namely, with the study of man's origins. The origin of man and his various societies constitutes a set of beliefs and ideas that is equally significant

15

to the theologian, the religious believer, the archaeologist, the anthropologist, the historian, the biologist, the geneticist, and so on. The ideas and beliefs relating to mankind's beginnings typically involve a commitment of considerable proportions on the part of the holder, and even the layman-on-the-street finds himself excited and challenged by new discoveries and ideas in this area. Beliefs and ideas about man's genesis have formed the basis of various religious and scientific systems, and it is a particularly fruitful area to illustrate the potent influence of tradition as a tool of the dominant social group.

At the same time, I cannot resist launching this venture with someone who is a pure shoo-in on any list of oddestballs. This first illustrative oddball qualifies on more counts than I care to number, but a cursory review of his offbeat credentials indicates they are quite in order. This man is the originator of the idea that God Himself was actually an ancient astronaut from another planet. This person is truly exemplary in the area of offbeat ideas, and his thesis goes on to state that you and I and the man-next-door are actually the descendants of a long-gone interbreeding experiment in which a colonial expedition of aliens from some distant planet intermated with the evolving apelike creatures of the planet Earth. Certainly, this represents a sufficient departure from the conventional ideas about man's prehistory to qualify as unmitigated oddballlitry. This strangely creative and unique thinker is quite obviously a self-taught man (I mean, who could teach him?), a genuine auto-didact bent on doing his own thing. At the same time, he is a pure amateur who has introduced immensely heated controversies into one of the most staid and reserved of professions. This is a man whose best-selling book was written while in prison, an observation he casually tosses off in the book's foreword, as though everyone writes their best-selling books while in prison.

Our first oddball is none other than Erich von Daniken, author of the remarkable *Chariots of the Gods?* In an introduction to another of his works, *Gods from Outer Space*, William Roggersdorf observes:

Erich von Daniken has the spontaneity of the enthusiast. In the summer of 1968 he read articles by Vlatcheslav Saizev in the Soviet journal *Sputnik* with titles such as "Spaceship in the Himalayas" and "Angels in Spaceships." Von Daniken booked a flight to Moscow on the spot. There Professor Shklovsky, director of the Radio Astronomic Department of the Soviet Academy of Science's Sternberg Institute, answered his questions.

The author of *Chariots of the Gods?* was barely nineteen years old when his curiosity drove him to Egypt where he hoped to track down the real meaning of some cuneiform inscriptions. Since his first journey in 1954, he hops on planes to clear up his theories the way we catch a bus. Thinking on the space scale as he does, distance means nothing to him so long as the goal of his journeys provides arguments for the impossible.[1]

Von Daniken was born in 1935 in Zofingen, Switzerland, and attended the College St. Michael in Fribourg from 1949 through 1954. The brief biographical sketch that appears in *Contemporary Authors* gives some small indication of his offbeat character. His professional identification is listed as a "hotel-keeper and writer of science fiction," which is a less than ordinary blending of vocations. It goes on to note that von Daniken claims to have been "working in archaeology and space travel for fifteen years," another unusual blending of interests, and he is quoted as deriving great pleasure from "travelling around the world, finding new answers." My suspicion is that he derives even greater pleasure from "upping" the establishment. In his writings, which are quite uneven and range from moments of captivating logic to outright flights of fancy, this Swiss hotel-keeper seldom misses an opportunity to berate the archaeological professionals for their seemingly myopic adherence to an immensely constrained *Weltanschauung*, and he reaps untold delight in finding new interpretations of traditional artifactual data.

Von Daniken's theory of the origins of human culture

fly in the face of an impressive body of detailed scientific evidence and opinion. His proposals appear as preposterous to the archaeological establishment as the green-cheese theory of the moon's composition would be to an astrophysicist. To the archaeological professionals, von Daniken is less a stumbling amateur than an outright fool, and his hypothesis of man's prehistory is treated with contempt. Why?

The science of antiquities is as yet a relatively young member of the forum of human knowledge and probably has its beginnings in J. J. Wincklemann's *History of the Art of Antiquity*, written in the 1760s during preliminary excavations at Pompeii and Herculaneum in Italy. Wincklemann's work is an orderly arrangement and objective description of a tremendous accumulation of antique findings taken from the slopes of Mount Vesuvius. Its magnificent depictions of the treasures of Pompeii aroused a sleeping interest in the cultures of antiquity and paved the way for a means of gaining understanding of them by means of the artifacts dug from the earth.

In the past few centuries, painstaking canons (conventions) of archaeological investigation have slowly been established in the cautious and conservative attempt to gain a clear picture of man's prehistory and ancient beginnings. The science of archaeology has slowly advanced an increasingly clear understanding of the dawn of human history and the nature of the various cultures that have preceded the written record. Although there are local feuds and ongoing minor disagreements among the professionals, there is a relatively solid consensus that man's early cultural history is composed of identifiable civilizations that had their beginnings in the great and fertile valleys of the Tigris and Euphrates, Indus, Nile, and Yellow Rivers, peopled by men and women much like you and me. Although the educated Western man of modern times tends to be actively conscious of the Judeo-Christian and Greco-Roman influence, he readily assumes that these great cultural influences were themselves derived from perhaps less developed but similarly composed previous civilizations, an unbroken line of descent and increasing cultural complexity.

In one form or another, the professional archaeologist adopts a position very similar to that advanced by Arnold Toynbee in his twelve-volume *A Study of History*. Toynbee labors mightily in the enumeration and classification of civilizations and successfully maintains the point of view that the history of mankind is one of continuity and succession, with human effort building on and adding to previous human effort. The idol of the intellectual marketplace is that of the ongoing achievements of successive human cultures. Man is thus understood as an identifiable, knowable quantity, connected by adamantine links of heritage and heredity to the men of ancient history and prehistory. When we read *The Odyssey*, then, we sense our connection, through Homer, to the men of ancient times who have preceded us but who are much like us. The interconnectedness of the human experience is thus an intergral and unassailable assumption of the social sciences. Whatever minor differences in conclusions might be reached, the centrality of man as the end-point and singular achievement of an ongoing evolutionary process is never questioned.

Only an oddball would question and attack the assumptions and conclusions of generation upon generation of mankind's brightest intellects. Enter von Daniken. Witness the blasphemous questioning of the interconnectedness of the human experiential fabric. See the linkages of man between man, of culture between culture, of age between age begin to break down. Observe the wrath of the offended.

Von Daniken's intellectual meanderings have brought him to a vastly different set of conclusions and interpretations regarding man's distant past. Where others have looked for the cohesive themes and threads of continuity, von Daniken has chosen to look for the little pieces of evidence that do not fit the hypothesis of a gradually evolving human culture. Von Daniken's eye is not held by artifactual panorama of the human impetus, which lies behind the rise and fall of the early civilizations. Von Daniken deals with the same data that everyone has available, but his search is for other clues, for the occasional inexplicable artifact and discordant finding. It is as though he is compelled to find alternate understandings and novel interpretations.

The Plain of Nazca in Peru is an archaeological site laden with quizzical markings. Archaeologists have again and again seen these markings to be the remains of Inca roads or possibly the representations of some unusual religious symbolism. Yet von Daniken sees here an early airport for alien spacecraft!

In a variety of drawings that have survived from several ancient civilizations, archaeological professionals have seen evidence of earlier man's artistic drives to represent the religious and cultural rudiments of his experience. Von Daniken has seen in the same drawings clearly depicted astronauts in fully developed spacesuits!

It is unnecessary to review here the many pieces of "evidence" that he cites in support of his own theory. It is sufficient to say that over and over von Daniken dips into the archaeological treasure troves to find there what he terms "the improbable world of the unexplained." He uses the unexplained to cull evidence for his own offbeat propositions and to attack and dispel the conventional world-view of archaeology. The position that von Daniken eventually fosters in order to explain his own selective set of evidence is the necessary postulation of the presence of a series of interplanetary visitations by aliens from other planets in man's deep and distant past. He cites the likelihood of experimental intermating between these superior alien life-forms and the somewhat-less-than-fully-human but evolving life-forms of our own planet earth. In von Daniken's view, then, present man is the offspring of these interplanetary visitors, and the civilizations of our distant past are seen to reflect the overriding influence and patronage of the celestial visitors. The veritable pantheon of Gods seen to occur with such amazing regularity in the cultures of ancient civilizations are to von Daniken no more than the wistful representations of the celestial and godlike aliens who came to earth in the mysterious long-ago. To this Swiss hotel-keeper, the very idea of God has its inception in the rudimentary and primeval experience of the godlike astronauts from outer space making an absolutely incredible impression on the unformed consciousness of the prehominid life-forms that were slowly evolving on earth prior to this heavenly intrusion. Thus, von Daniken does not miss the opportunity to kill two birds with one stone, and his theory is equally offensive to both the scientific and religiously inclined.

The Danikenian viewpoint considerably alters the accepted scientific premise of massive evolutionary progression and continued development from primitive life-forms to urban metropolis. According to his view, the highest achievements of human culture are not due to man's progressive unfolding but rather to an external input of alien intelligence. Although many respectable scientists have entertained the prospect of intelligent and more advanced life on other planets as well as the possibility of interplanetary travel, von Daniken has taken the bold step and has drawn together the implications of these notions. In addition, he has attempted to set forth some "evidence," however sketchy it might be, to support his bold hypothesis.

It is not these aspects alone, however, that lead us to designate von Daniken as a genuine candidate for the society of oddballs. Granted that his theory is mildly original and sufficiently offbeat. It is, perhaps, also quite deflating to mankind's view of itself as pulling itself up by its bootstraps. There is something about the presentation of his theory that propels von Daniken into the realm of genuine iconoclasm. Von Daniken cannot resist displaying his own individuality and raising his finger in symbolic gesture to the established conventions.

Whatever the eventual merits of von Daniken's theory

of interplanetary intervention and mutation of human evolution, he does provide a strikingly different interpretation of a significant area of human thought and investigation. In a series of books, his hypothesis gathers energy from many sources in an attempt to bring his argument into sharper perspective. There can be no doubt, however, as to his underlying feeling that he has seen with a larger vision what other investigators have failed to see at all. At the same time, he senses his own self-importance: "I believe in the disturbing power of ideas that cannot be hushed up."[2] Von Daniken is, at times, consumed by his own drive for individualized expression:

> The classical method of research into antiquity has got bogged down and so cannot come to the right unassailable kind of conclusions. It is far too attached to its stereotyped pattern of thought and leaves no scope for the imaginative ideas and speculations which alone could produce a creative impulse.[3]

And again:

> It seems as if narrow-mindedness was always a special characteristic when new worlds of ideas were beginning. But on the threshold of the twenty-first century the research worker should be prepared for fantastic realities. He should be eager to revise laws and knowledge which were considered sacrosanct for centuries but are nevertheless called in question by new knowledge. Even if a reactionary army tries to damn up this new intellectual flood, a new world must be conquered in the teeth of all the unteachable, in the name of truth and reality.[4]

There is in these statements a strong hint of the zealot as well as the iconoclast. Von Daniken is furious at the smug complacence of conventional wisdom and the idolatrous nature of intellectual tradition. In a particularly heated passage, he maintains:

We have a thousand and one past errors to correct. The self-assurance that is feigned is threadbare and is really only an acute form of stubbornness. At the conference tables of orthodox scientists the delusion still prevails that a thing must be proved before a "serious" person may—or can—concern himself with it.

In the past the man who put forward a brand-new idea had to count on being despised and persecuted by the church and his colleagues. Things must have become easier, one thinks. There are no more anathemas, and fires at the stake are no longer lighted. The snag is that the methods of our time are less spectacular, but they are hardly less obstructive to progress. Now everything is more "civilized" and there is much less fuss. Theories and intolerably audacious ideas are hushed up or dismissed by such killer phrases as:

It's against the rules! (Always a good one!)

It's not classical enough! (Bound to impress.)

It's not revolutionary! (Unequaled in its deterrent effect!)

The universities won't go along with that! (Convincing!)

Others have already tried that! (Of course. But were they successful?)

We can't see any sense in it! (And that's that!)

That hasn't been proved yet! *(Quod erat demonstrandum!)*[5]

Von Daniken's thirst for the novel and the different is inextricably intertwined with an indictment of the sponsors of the tried and true, and he has little patience with the wisdom of the ages. Under the rubric of the search for truth, he is willing and eager to discard the accumulated judgments of previous investigators as a block to the development of new knowledge. In all honesty, however, it must be pointed out that he is quite selective with traditional wisdom and is more than happy to embrace those aspects of tradition that support his own unique vision. In the final analysis, it is his own unique theory that he seeks to support and his own individuality that he wishes to foster and preserve.

It is yet too early for the workings of traditional and ongoing methods of knowledge-gathering to separate the wheat from the chaff in the von Daniken theory. Perhaps his vision of historical interstellar visitation will prove one day to be little more than a finely etched grotesquerie. On the other hand, it might well stimulate subsequent investigators and theorizers to more integrated perspectives on the complex nature of the universe. Von Daniken's unusual interest in archaeology and space travel and the conclusions to which this interest has brought him might well form the basis of the conventional wisdom of the future.

The fate of his vision is in the hands of time, but his penchant for bold statement and heated controversy has brought him considerable attention. Von Daniken's maverick quality is best seen not only in the display of an unusual idea but also in his eagerness to use that idea to prod the consciousness and ruffle the feathers of those who man the status quo. It should be pointed out that it is not necessary for the creator of an original theory to use his theory to pique the Establishment.

We will turn our attention now to a man of unquestioned creativity, originality, and genius who is nonetheless immensely sensitive to and tied into the traditions of his time. Remaining in this same area of ideas about the origin of mankind, we will investigate a man who has proposed one of the truly revolutionary ideas in history, but who was also a man who had profound respect for the established traditions of his age.

3 Charles Darwin

The Monkeys in Our Genes

HIS INITIAL SORTIE into oddballitry has focused on a particular area of human thought, namely the sets of hypotheses, evidence, and beliefs dealing with the nature of man's origins and history. In effect, we are attempting to illustrate the workings of tradition by studying the notion of tradition. The historical implications about man's culture and beliefs about the derivation of man himself are central to the consideration of convention and tradition, the generation-by-generation management of what has been handed down and handed on. Man's understanding of his origin is a peculiarly sacred dimension of convention, seeming to demand a considerable degree of reverence and respect.

Charles Robert Darwin (1809-1882), the English naturalist, has unquestionably been more influential than any other thinker in revising a tradition of understanding and belief regarding the origin of mankind. The educated layman in the contemporary world is trained on Darwin as a matter of course. Darwin is everywhere regarded as the father of

25

modern evolutionary theory and his influence on the human and biological sciences is so far-reaching that it is well-nigh impossible to dwell on man's nature without Darwinian perspective. The convention-attacking von Daniken, for example, must assume Darwin as the point of departure for his own offbeat meanderings.

It was a far different intellectual and religious climate, however, that formed the ambiance of Darwin's own investigations and theorizing. It is quite true that several influential predecessors and contemporaries of Darwin had flirted with the notion of evolutionary unfolding and descent. Darwin's own grandfather, Erasmus Darwin (1731-1802), had previously suggested the main lines of Darwin's eventual theory. In this respect, there was a certain paving of the way for Darwin's revolutionary theory. But as Waddington has tersely remarked, "For everyone, except perhaps a few pedantic historians, the 'Theory of Evolution' means 'Darwin' as unmistakably as 'Relativity' means 'Einstein.'"[1]

At the time of Darwin, the dominant theory of man's origin was the Judeo-Christian doctrine of creationism, a belief which lay at the very heart of all Western European religions. The doctrine of creationism maintains that the "furniture of the universe," every species of plant and animal, man himself, is the product of the direct, creative activity of God, particularly as set forth in the all-at-once creation account in the book of Genesis. To deny this belief was, and for many still is, tantamount to an attack on the entire fabric of man's religious experience and the very basis of human moral existence. Darwin himself was singularly aware of the apparent clash and contradiction of the theory he was forming and the ardent religious aspirations of the society in which he lived. And Charles Darwin was very much a man of convention.

The son of a widowed country doctor, Darwin, in his early years, had succumbed to his father's wish that he also practice medicine. Despite his own passion for natural history, young Darwin entered the Edinburgh University for his medical training. He was unhappy in medical school, however, and with his father's blessing he eventually enrolled in Christ's College, Cambridge, with the intention of ultimately becoming a priest. While at Cambridge, Darwin fell under the influence of the Reverend Professor John S. Henslow, who would one day recommend that Darwin be the naturalist on the voyage of the H.M.S. *Beagle*. It was on this extended voyage of the *Beagle* (1831-1836), which literally sailed around the world, that Darwin began gathering the extensive evidence for his theory of the evolutionary development of species.[2]

Whereas von Daniken was shown to be eager for the limelight and turmoil of public controversy, Darwin was exceedingly anxious to eschew any hint of unorthodoxy. In many respects, Darwin's ideas were much more revolutionary for his age than are von Daniken's in relation to the mid-twentieth century freedom of intellectual dissent. Darwin's consciousness of the religious and scientific convictions of his peers led him to extreme caution in the sharing of his findings and ideas. When he learned that his friend Henslow had printed some extracts from his letters, he wrote his sister Catherine: "I have been a good deal horrified by a sentence in your letter where you talk of 'the little book with the extracts from your letters.' I can only suppose they refer to a few geological details. But I have always written to Henslow in the same careless manner as to you, and to print what has been written without care or accuracy is indeed playing with edged tools."[3]

Whereas von Daniken's personality and style are as flamboyant as his ideas, Darwin was a conservative, well-lettered man seldom given to any form of self-indulgence. Whereas von Daniken delights in displays of his own individualistic spirit, Darwin found sufficient creativity in the scientific statement of his findings and his ideas. And yet, Darwin's findings and ideas were considerably more outrageous to his age than are the wildest flights of fancy engaged in by von Daniken. Despite his conservative nature, Darwin's theory is genuine oddballitry when considered in the intellectual and religious framework of his environment. Or was it? What enabled Darwin to arrive at a set of conclusions apparently so disparate from the accepted ideas of his day?

In 1859, Darwin published his most famous work, *On the Origin of Species by Means of Natural Selection*, a highly scientific but nonetheless readable book whose salient ideas were counter to the creationist theology of his Christian upbringing. It will be recalled that a central belief of the creationist account maintains that each species of plant and animal was brought into being by a separate act of God, the Creator. To the extent, then, that plant and animal species remain distinctly different from each other, the story of the creation as set forth in the Old Testament is certainly a reasonable account of how living things had come into existence. In *The Origin of Species*, Darwin gathered a convincing array of factual data indicating that various species of plant and animal life do change over time, and he advanced the "principle of natural selection" as an identifiable, biological mechanism by which such change takes place. In other words, Darwin built a solid case explaining the bewildering assemblage of existing forms of plant and animal life as having evolved in time from similar but distinct groupings of ancestors. This theory undeniably contradicts the literal statement of creation developed in the book of Genesis.

C. H. Waddington tersely states the implication of these findings:

> For instance, in the isolated archipelago of the Galápagos Islands, Darwin found a number of species of a kind of bird usually referred to as a "finch," although it was not identical with the British bird of that name. The Galápagos finch-species are not found anywhere else, and although they are quite well-defined, separate species, these share many features with each other. This is just what one would expect if they had all originated

within the archipelago by divergence from a single ancestral species which had in some way once suc-ceeded in reaching that isolated locality. Looking at a large number of such cases, Darwin argued that an ex-planation in terms of evolution is more convincing than the alternative, which supposes that the existing species have been specifically created to exhibit geographical distributions and morphological relationships of some apparent regularity which are, however, quite meaning-less. It is, of course, difficult to guess what the ways of a Creator would be, but it would be nothing less than blas-phemous to accuse him of building into his creation apparent clues to an underlying pattern which was in reality non-existent.[4]

It would be a mistake to understate the controversial effects of Darwin's theory on the intellectual order of his time. And yet, in this earthshaking volume, Darwin had no more than alluded to the prospect of man himself as a similar evo-lutionary phenomenon. It was clear that Darwin was taking great pains to avoid ruffling unnecessarily the feathers of his readers. He was not interested in controversy, and he actively sought to dispel the prospect of emotional biases in-terfering with the dispassionate presentation of his findings.

For this reason, he did not publish his *Descent of Man* until 1871. In the words of Le Gros Clark:

In the introduction to the first edition of *The Descent of Man*, Darwin specifically stated that he had for many years been collecting notes on this subject, not with the intention of publishing them, "but rather with the deter-mination not to publish," as he thought by so doing he would only add to the prejudices against his general con-clusions regarding the evolutionary process.[5]

Again and again, we see in Darwin the caution of a reserved spirit compelled by the evidence that he surveys to rewrite man's understanding of himself, but nonetheless aware of the impact of his thinking on the established systems of belief. Darwin continued to have serious qualms about the publication of this volume, and in the second edition he makes reference to the "fiery ordeal" through which the first edition had passed.

It is *The Descent of Man*, of course, that clearly established Darwin as the father of "the monkey theory." The implications of man's own descent from other forms of primate species were clearly present in *Origin of Species*, but it was in *Descent* that the beginning evidence for human evolution was honed into a workable viewpoint. Le Gros Clark refers to the publication of this work as "an act of great moral courage," indicating the tremendous risk that Darwin ran in explicating a theory so counter to man's established understanding of himself. In America, "the monkey theory" received extensive national publicity in the early 1920s when Clarence Darrow locked horns with William Jennings Bryan in the now infamous Scopes Trial. The brilliant and conservative Bryan had a veritable field day mocking the proposition that man could have possibly been descended from the same species as apes. It should further be pointed out that the evidence for man's biological evolution today is incredibly more extensive than the few intimations with which Darwin had to work; and yet, there are many today who continue to view "the theory of evolution" as a monstrous work of evil. Such is the power of time-honored traditions!

What, then, enabled Darwin to risk the stigma of religious heresy and even social opprobrium in order to bring together the threads and themes of evolutionary theory? Bentley Glass, coauthor of a book on the forerunners of Darwin, makes the following observation:

> Thus, as the individual often resolves an implacable conflict by repressing it into the subconscious, so human thought in the first half of the nineteenth century stubbornly and blindly repressed the implications of the

growing evidence in regard to the origin of species, including his own. Darwin was the outburst of those
repressed conclusions, the victory of that submerged
scientific conviction. His was the magnificent synthesis
of evidence, all known before, and of theory, adum-
brated in every postulate by his forerunners—a synthesis so compelling in honesty and comprehensiveness
that it forced such men as Thomas Henry Huxley to say:
How stupid not to have realized that before![6]

Despite this crystallization of the scientific impetus in
the person of Darwin, the Darwinian theory remained un-
realized by his predecessors for good reason, namely that it
was sufficiently offbeat, in terms of the times, to run the risk
of being outright screwiness. The suggestion of man's co-
origin with the monkeys, no matter how compelling the
scientific evidence might be, was so far beyond the scope of
the man-in-the-street that only an oddball could advance
such a position and expect to be believed! What, then, was
the source of the moral courage which inspired Darwin to
pursue his theory in the public forum? The publication of his
work was obviously intended to convert others to his own
point of view and thus to expose himself as well to the casti-
gations and calumnies of the uninitiated and unsympathetic.
What was Darwin up to?

Whatever the risks of public ridicule, and they were
unquestionably considerable, the English naturalist was
nonetheless committed to the pursuit of his unique vision.
Darwin's ability to run the gauntlet of "the fiery ordeal" and to
step beyond the pale of orthodoxy is only partially illumin-
ated by the notion that his work stands as "the victory of the
submerged scientific conviction." It is true that evolution was
in the air and that evolutionary implications formed much of
the *Zeitgeist* of his era. For this reason, *Origin* and *Descent*
were neither the first blow nor the coup de grace to a view of
the world and an understanding of man that had apparently
stood without serious challenge for many, many centuries,

albeit with much more vigor and enforced acceptance in the centuries immediately preceding Darwin. And yet, it was Darwin who brought this new viewpoint to fruition.

There is no need to conduct an in-depth personality analysis of Darwin himself, but I would like to draw attention to the early threads and themes that were present in his education and development. It is my suspicion that Darwin was enabled to bring his new vision to fruition precisely because he sensed that his theory was *not* counter to the essentials of man's moral and religious traditions! I believe that Darwin likely felt comfortable with the prospect of a genuine integration of traditions, of the older tradition of religious creationism and of his own developing tradition of scientific evolutionism. I am saying that Darwin was quite probably alert to the prospect of a Hegelian dialectic in which a new idea runs squarely into an old idea to produce a merger of the old and the new.

It should be recalled that Erasmus Darwin, the grand-father of Charles, had laid the groundwork for this eventuality. In *Zoonomia*, written between 1794 and 1796, the elder Darwin had speculated on the notion of an embryo-state universe created gradually and over long periods of time by an involved creator. Grandfather Darwin boldly imagined that millions of ages before the beginning of man, all warm-blooded animals arose from some one living source endowed by the First Cause (God) with animality, with the power of acquiring new parts and forms as well as the power of de-livering these new forms generation upon generation to posterity. Is it not likely that Charles was sympathetic to the inchoate vision of his own grandfather and that he was well aware of the likelihood of a more complete interface between the apparent discrepancies of evolutionism and creationism? It should further be recalled that throughout his life, Darwin had the enthusiastic support of one of the shining lights of Christ's College, Cambridge, namely the aforementioned Reverend Professor Henslow. Did not Darwin sense the prospect of eventual support from the intellectual, scientific, and religious establishment through the very person of the man Henslow who embodied these traditions of understanding within himself?

Darwin's contributions are now a century past, and the judgment of history has served to sanction his brilliance and to honor his considerable contributions to man's understanding of himself. The Bible-thumping fundamentalists who disagree with Darwin are now likely to be considered the oddballs. At the same time, there are deeper lessons to be learned from the man Darwin. In retrospect, it is clear that this particular oddball was not crazy and that his "weird ideas" were no more than the logic of a larger view. If he has seen farther than other men, it is likewise true that he has stood on the shoulders of giants. But to the rank and file of his own age, Darwin was undoubtedly a madman and a weirdo.

The Darwinian revolution in ideas is no longer shocking, and even the creationist theology called into question by Darwin's finding has now achieved a seemingly comfortable synthesis. The religious believer continues to see the hand of God providently involved in the continuing works of creation, and science itself poses less and less a threat to the man of traditional faith. Nonetheless, as more and more of mankind are exposed to secular education and the urbane sophistication of modern science, it is the originators of the pre-scientific traditions that are more and more being seen as the freaks and the oddballs. In the following pages, we will continue exploring this area of human thought having to do with the nature of man's origins, but we will lay back the passage of time to an oddball who lived long before Darwin and who, it seems, set in motion the dynamics of the very tradition that Darwin was to work against.

Before leaving Darwin, however, it is worth noting that one can be an oddball without being completely anticonventional. Darwin illustrates the case of a man whose beliefs are in apparent violation of a set of traditions held by a large segment of his own social group but at the same time whose apparently offbeat ideas are supported and encouraged by an increasing minority within the same larger social grouping. His intent was not to disrupt tradition but rather to pursue and see through the ramifications of his own emergent views. The support of fellow scientists served to encourage Darwin's own individuality and his need to achieve a point of view suitable to the compelling evidence of his own investigations. The allegiance to the rudimentary notions of his grandfather and the response to the gentle promptings and suggestions of his friend Henslow acted as catalysts in his own unique quest. Nor is Darwin's individuality diminished in any way by the fact that others in his own time shared similar ideas; he is now considered the father of an established set of scientific traditions and ideas regarding the origin of man.

4 Moses Speaks
"And the Lord Said to Moses..."

THE CREATIONIST THEOLOGY to which I have referred somewhat sketchily is the product of an extensive history of tradition—building into the Judeo-Christian ethic. In the epoch immediately preceding the era of Darwin, this theological perspective had been subjected to the dogmatic sanctions of the established churches. In Reformation and Counterreformation Europe, religious intolerance and zealotry had more than occasionally rendered orthodoxy of belief and expression a matter of life or death. At times, it appeared that freedom *from* religion was even more humane than freedom *of* religion. At any rate, the religious wars of the sixteenth and seventeenth centuries had brought the question of adherence to specific traditions into very sharp focus, and men had learned to be very particular and cautious about the nature of their beliefs.

The various Christian credos, both Catholic and Protestant, as well as the Jewish faith, were oddly united on the matter of man's origins. Although the various faiths differed considerably on many fundamentals, they tended to maintain similar postures regarding their beliefs about the origin of humankind. All the major religions of the West had maintained the essential view of the Biblical account of creation set forth in the book of Genesis. The various religions likewise continued the traditional belief that this account of creation had been inspired by God and written by the hand of Moses. Moses, who probably died in the twelfth century B.C., is clearly one of the most widely read and influential authors in history, and in many respects he must be considered *the* father of Western traditions. In the Jewish faith, he is credited with the authorship of the Torah, the books of the law that form the basis of Judaism. In the various Christian religions, these same materials are known as the Pentateuch, the first five books of the Old Testament (Genesis, Exodus, Leviticus, Numbers, and Deuteronomy) and are equally basic to the central beliefs of Christianity.

These sacred books of the Judeo-Christian religious and cultural tradition are often referred to as Mosaic history. This history begins with the account of God's creation of the world in seven days, the story of Adam and Eve, Noah and the flood, the foundation of the Hebrew people through the leadership of the patriarch Abraham, the exodus from captivity in Egypt, and so forth. These books are written in a variety of forms including stories, epics, poems, and legal codes. The combined collection is hardly the work of a single writer and instead bears the stamp of many. It concludes with the death and burial of Moses, the account of which was hardly written by Moses himself. Even a man of Moses' considerable abilities would have had difficulty describing his own funeral.

Scriptural scholars enter into a variety of disagreements about Moses' authorship of these sacred texts. He certainly did not write these books in the sense of a modern author who takes pen and paper in hand and begins jotting down his thoughts. Modern scriptural scholars feel quite certain that most of the material contained in these books was actually written down long after Moses' death, down through the fifth century B.C. It is believed today that the actual text of the Pentateuch is composed of at least four different major oral traditions, which were communicated from generation to generation for many centuries before their actual commission to a written text by a number of later writers.[1] Thus, Moses is said to be the author of these books in the sense that he is the great teacher, inspired by God to provide his people the religious meaning of their lives. Even when the later writers wrote about events said to have taken place before Moses, they did so only under the influence of his doctrine and considerable teachings. The picture of the spirit of God whispering in the ear of Moses as he sits at his desk taking down word-by-word account is obviously quite a travesty.

It is unfortunate that the history of established religions typically finds subsequent authorities idealizing the founders and casting the teachings in thunderbolts and cement blocks. At the time of Darwin, for example, much credence was placed in the writings of Archbishop Ussher who treated the Mosaic history as a literal chronological account. Writing in the 1660s, Ussher actually counted all the "begats" and ages of the patriarchs as set forth in the Mosaic account. He concluded that the divinely revealed *date* of creation could be safely placed in the year 4004 B.C. Ussher is another example of the genuine fanatic for tradition and literal law whom changing traditions have cast in the role of genuine oddball!

Let us return, however, to the character of Moses and the nature of his teachings. In point of fact, we know nothing about the man except for the material that is contained in the Mosaic history, and this is hardly autobiographical. Those of us who have been exposed to Charlton Heston, Cecil B. DeMille, and *The Ten Commandments* might well have clear and concise pictures in our mind's eye but I doubt that Moses himself could have been nearly as regal and self-important as Heston himself. And yet, he must surely have been an unusual man. What we are here referring to as a genuine oddball!

After twenty centuries of Christianity, we are accustomed to believing that, prior to Darwin, man always understood his beginnings in the manner described in the Genesis story of God's creation, which is now seen as a kind of religious statement of cosmic and human origins. In point of fact, the Hebrews were only one of a larger group of Semitic peoples who circulated a veritable verbal library of myths and tales about the creation of the world. The Semitic tribes were a polytheistic group, and there were many versions of different gods being active in the foundation of the human race. Contemporary religious credos now accept the belief that God made a special revelation to Abraham in the nineteenth century B.C., the essence of which was that there is but one God who was the creator of the cosmos and of man. The polytheistic creation myths of the Semitic peoples were then rethought and sifted through the best minds of succeeding generations. The monotheistic creation story of Genesis, then, is the culmination of inspired theological thought over centuries of time in which pagan myths were reworked in order to state the religious revelation of the one, true God, the God of Abraham, and truer yet, the God of Moses. Chapters 12 through 50 of the Book of Genesis, which is literally the book of beginnings, quickly leap from the dawn of history to describe the national origins of the Hebrew People. The nonbeliever may well see here the incredible *chutzpah* of a small nomadic tribe which sanctions its national destiny by arrogating to itself the unique support and seal of approval of the all-powerful God. At the very least, the creation story of Genesis serves to trace a direct line of descent between God's special intervention in the creation of the first man, Adam, and his continuing intervention in behalf of

Adam's descendants, thus forming the current nation of the Hebrews. Although this creation story expresses the interconnectedness of all mankind as descendants of Adam, it is also a candid statement of the priority of the Hebrew nation.

There seems here a considerable lesson on the nature of traditions. Traditions are not sacred solely because they are time-honored and long-standing. They have the power to shape the adherence of the social group precisely because they lend a special meaning and advantage to that social group. In the case of the Hebrews, the traditions served then as well as now to designate a special, preemptive situation and signal the importance of the group itself. The creation story, for example, enabled the Hebrews to sense their special calling from God, and it is for such reasons that the creation traditions assumed a sacred nature. The Genesis account of God's direct intervention in the creation of man and the cosmos acts as a foundation for a continuing history of God's direct intervention and providence for the social group. It is the person of Moses who best typifies the nature of that nation's relationship to the power of God. Moses is the man who speaks to God face to face. What Moses says comes directly from God. What more formidable sanction could one ask for "doing it my way"?

In the Pentateuch, Moses is regularly described as a pipeline between God and the man-in-the-street. Mosaic history, as recounted in the first five books of the Old Testament, is regularly punctuated with the statement, "And the Lord told Moses. . . . " For example, in the Exodus statement of the proclamation of the Ten Commandments, there is the following preamble:

> On the morning of the third day there were peals of thunder and lightning, and a heavy cloud over the mountain, and a very loud trumpet blast, so that all the people in the camp trembled. But Moses led the people out of the camp to meet God, and they stationed themselves at the foot of the mountain. Mount Sinai was all

wrapped up in smoke, for the Lord came down upon it in fire. The smoke rose from it as though from a furnace, and the whole mountain trembled violently. The trumpet blast grew louder and louder, while Moses was speaking and God answered him with thunder.

When the Lord came down to the top of Mount Sinai, he summoned Moses to the top of the mountain, and Moses went up to him. Then the Lord told Moses, "Go down and warn the people not to break through toward the Lord in order to see him; otherwise many of them will be struck down. The priests, too, who approach the Lord must sanctify themselves; else he will vent his anger upon them." Moses said to the Lord, "The people cannot go up to Mount Sinai, for you yourself warned us to set limits around the mountain to make it sacred." The Lord repeated, "Go down now! Then come up again along with Aaron. But the priests and the people must not break through to come up to the Lord; else he will vent his anger upon them." So Moses went down to the people and told them this. (Exodus, 19: 16-25)

There then follows the statement of the covenant or alliance between God and the nation, the central portion of which is the Ten Commandments and the main portion of which is an extensive network of injunctions and prohibitions that codifies every aspect of daily existence.

The actual character of Moses, of course, is shrouded in history, but the Biblical account clearly recognizes him as a great teacher who speaks to the people for God and who speaks to God for the people. He is, in fact, not only a great emancipator who led his people to the edge of freedom from their bondage in Egypt, he is also the first of the great tradition-breakers and tradition-makers. From the various religious creeds, forms of worship, social and legal codes that formed the cultural environment of the Semitic people, Moses was to father a highly refined statement of moral, social, and religious expectations and to sanction the same as the word of God. Again and again, Mosaic history recounts the ordeal of Moses in attempting to alter the ongoing pattern of idol worship and pagan ritual to which his people had been accustomed. Moses' task was to develop a new set of traditions, a superior understanding of the nation and its meaning, and in this effort he was constantly disappointed in the tendency of his people to fall back into the worship of idols and the attendant polytheistic rituals. He obviously felt these produced an inferior and self-defeating understanding of life and destiny.

Mircea Eliade, in his remarkable analysis of the ontology of premodern societies, makes the following observation:

> If we observe the general behavior of archaic man, we are struck by the following fact: neither the objects of the external world or human acts, properly speaking, have any autonomous intrinsic value. Objects or acts acquire a value, and in so doing become real, because they participate, after one fashion or another, in a reality that transcends them. . . .
>
> In the particulars of his conscious behavior, the "primitive," the archaic man, acknowledges no act which has not been previously posited and lived by someone else, some other being who was not a man. What he does has been done before. His life is the ceaseless repetition of gestures initiated by others.[2]

Eliade draws attention to the unconscious, formative meaning of tradition, for the primitive as well as the modern, but his designation of the mechanisms of traditional thought, of the deeper meaning of repetitive patterns, is especially illuminating to this analysis of Mosaic tradition.

The Mosaic history attempts to recast the ordinary, historical development of the Hebrews by assigning a special significance and transcendental meaning to the sanctioned customs of the tribe. The commonplace, everyday rituals and customs, the very character and quality of the day-by-day activities of the people, are elevated to a higher meaning because these events are sanctioned and prescribed by the one God. Moses produced a finely detailed code which covered every conceivable aspect of daily life, a code which raised the level of meaning of every prosaic activity because the code itself emanated from a covenant, an agreement between God and the people.

Thus, Moses has come down to posterity as a law-maker and law-giver, and he is known as the authoritative transmitter of divine law. It is assuredly true that the Mosaic Law is a blanket that renders human experience decidedly common, enforcing a repetitive, cyclical, and easily agreed-upon aspect to the experience of the many. And yet, the enduring qualities of Moses' contribution to human religion also bear the stamp of his highly individualized spirit and personality. It is the ontologic-mystical-transcendent meaning of these traditions that provided a genuinely new emphasis and impetus to man's developing religious consciousness.

The Biblical portrayal of Moses smashing the pagan idols is signal evidence of his oddball individuality. He would tolerate no god other than Yahweh, the God of his experience. He is a disrupter of the existing traditions and an antagonist of the common view and traditional practices. His lasting contribution to and continuing influence on religion are in his own unique statement of monotheism, his experience of a unique God who is the creator of all things, the source of all justice, and the transcendent meaning of human activity. Granted that Hebrew monotheism is a religious belief that did not reach its full theological fruition until long after Moses. Nonetheless, the seeds may be found in the highly individualized experience of Moses himself. As Harold Rowley has pointed out:

> . . . the religious achievement of Moses was not something that grew naturally out of his environment or circumstances, and the ideas that he mediated to Israel were not derived from Egypt or from any other place. Certainly they were not ideas that were floating around

in that age. "The real source of Hebrew monotheism,"
says Wardle, "we should probably find in the religious
experience of Moses. . . . "[3]

Moses' unique contribution was to relate the God of creation
to the God of Sinai to the God of everyday life, and it is in this
respect that he fostered a new impulse to man's understanding of religion. It is the interconnectedness and universality of
Moses' God, Yahweh, that designates a new religious meaning. This God is everywhere and has been for all time. He is
the only God and there is none other like him. And he spoke
through Moses.

No doubt, subsequent writers of the Old Testament
considerably embellished the character of the man Moses as
well as the events for which he is famous. The feats of Moses
likely increased and multiplied with each recounting of the
tale, and yet he still remains an innovative and deeply creative
thinker and leader who must have been thought very, very
weird by his peers and colleagues. The traditions that grew
from him are just as surely a function of the burst of his own
individuality and rare experience with his God. The ability of
Moses to find a larger meaning for his life and to extend this
meaning to the members of his social group must have
rendered him quite suspect to the polytheistic conventionalists and tradition-bearers of his day. One suspects that he
would surely have encountered many disbelievers in his
public proclamations of his conversations with the Godhead,
and his dangerous beliefs must have alarmed the city fathers.
And yet, Moses struck out for the novel view and followed
the promptings of his own spirit, whether of God or not.
Despite his subsequent designation as "lawgiver" and "father
of traditions," Moses unquestionably stood apart from the
common experiences of his fellow Hebrews. In his day and
age, he must have been oddball dynamite.

This brief study of Moses also will serve our own
coming transition from the intellectually creative oddball to
the genuine social innovator. In this cursory description of

some important oddballs in the history of ideas regarding man's origin, we have perhaps underlined the break from intellectual traditions and the power of ideas. When dealing with ideas, of course, innovation and change are represented by the development of new ideas and/or novel ideological systems. Moses, nonetheless, was both thinker and behaver, a genuine smasher of idols. In the next section, we will turn our attention much more directly to the behavior of oddballs, rather than to their ideas alone.

Part Two

Outrageous Behavior and the Prospect of Change

5 Diogenes of Sinope

The Philosopher-Dog Who Lived in a Tub

THE OFTTIMES BRILLIANT, sometimes weird, but never oddball, German philosopher G.W.F. Hegel (1770-1831) viewed the dynamics of thinking and the history of ideas as a kind of dialectical process in which an existing idea would eventually meet or even generate an opposing idea with the consequent friction between the opposing notions eventually producing a blend of the contrasting notions. Hegel summarized this process as thesis-antithesis-synthesis, and he considered this dialectical juxtaposition to be an enduring characteristic of individual minds as well as mind itself.

For example, albeit oversimplified, using the notion of private property, the following process might well be described. At some point in the life of some social group, those who have come to acquire property (the haves) might well set forth the idea that the individual person has a right to the property he has acquired and should be so protected by the social group. On the other hand, as those who do not own property (the have-nots) become disenchanted with their lot, an opposing idea might come to vogue, namely that all property should be held in common by the social group for use by all members. Over the course of time, a series of compromises, clarifications, distinctions, and refinements of the general idea of private vs. common property would be effectuated (the have-somes).In this way, the philosophy and law of social economics, as well as the daily exigencies of the group members, are subject to an ongoing process of dialectical change, in which the established notions are pitted against developing and novel points of view. From the Hegelian view, then, I would maintain that oddballs are necessarily written into the process of dialectical change. Hegel himself could never make it as pure oddball, however, as he believed in the peculiarly German mania concerning obedience to the law. Philosophically, he maintained that Mind establishes law, morality, and the state, which he saw as a society of free individuals who willingly accept the laws and customs of the people. Oddballs, as we are beginning to see, typically sense a greater degree of disparity between the individual and the social group.

At the same time, human and social change involve far more than the evolution of ideas. Philosophers and theoreticians traffic almost exclusively in ideas, the very tools of their trade. Since they tend to write most of the books, thought itself is often overemphasized as the salient characteristic of human endeavor. Karl Marx (1818-1883), for example, was able to translate Hegel's abstract dialectic into a concrete, practical dialectic, which constitutes, in effect, a format and prospectus for social revolution. Marx remained, however, very much an ivory-tower specialist in the art of ideas, and the application of his works has merely tended to champion one form of social constitution over another. Marx, like Hegel, could never gain entrance into any Top Ten listing of oddballs.

From my own developing point of view, I would be quite disinclined to limit the oddball to ideas alone. Not every weirdo is captivated solely by the pleasures of abstract speculation, and many more oddballs are simply inclined to go out and do. In point of fact, the arena of behavior is an amazingly fertile field for the demonstration of individuality. The violation of the conventions of acceptable behavior is likewise more likely to produce greater howls of upset from the maintainers of the status quo than could possibly be accomplished by means of a weird idea alone. In the coming chapters, we will investigate a few very special oddballs who have distinguished themselves in the arena of outrageous behavior. They are men of ideas as well, but they are especially unique in the ability to translate the outlandish idea into the flagrant act. Each in his own way has been a philosopher of social change and societal reform, but, more importantly for our present purposes, each has seen fit to dramatize his ideas of social change by well-turned feats of unconventionality.

The award as the Philosophical and Behavioral Father of Oddballitry goes hands down and unquestionably so to none other than Diogenes of Sinope (412-323 B.C.). Diogenes was a student of Socrates, once removed and through the mediation of Antisthenes, the founder of the Cynic school of which Diogenes was to become its most individualized proponent. He was likewise a contemporary of Plato and Aristotle, the very fonts of Greek wisdom and the parents of philosophical enterprise in the Western world. In short, Diogenes moved in a pretty fast company and could hold his own with the great ones.

It should be remembered that the Athens of 461 B.C. was one of the most intellectually productive centers and periods in Western history. The shadow and influence of Socrates, who had been forced to drink the hemlock at the hands of the city fathers (on the very real charge of corrupting the minds of the youth), stimulated a veritable beehive of discussion and reflection. Socrates, "the gadfly of Athens," stood as the personification of man's search for truth, asserting the rights of free inquiry, questioning men of reputation and position, remaining steadfast in the face of opposition. Eventually, he was convicted by convention.

With the example of Socrates to nudge his own

becoming, Diogenes was to test completely the inborn tensions between the life of the virtuous, individualizing man and the customs of the social group. He was a man committed to unearthing the folly of custom and the vices of the social order. It is reported that when somebody asked him, "What sort of man do you consider Diogenes to be?" he replied, "Socrates gone mad."[1] In other words, Diogenes was Socrates gone completely and beautifully oddball, and his life will stand forever as the classic demonstration of the individualizing self versus the conventionalizing social group.

There is good evidence that Diogenes was an unexceptionable scoundrel in his youth. His biographer, Diogenes Laertius, has bequeathed posterity a wondrous collection of anecdotes and sayings, and he begins his tale with the note that Diogenes was driven into exile from his native city of Sinope, allegedly for having adulterated the coinage, no mean feat, of course, for a fledgling philosopher. A natural table-turner, when late in his life someone reminded him that he had been sentenced to exile by the people of Sinope, he quickly replied, "Yes, and I sentenced them to staying home."[2] He had a marvelous knack, it seems, for landing on his feet. Leaving Sinope in apparent haste, he then came to Athens and soon outstripped the masters in the living of philosophy.

One of the central themes in the teachings of Socrates was the living of the virtuous life. Socrates had maintained that the purpose of life was to live well, and he was renowned for the sayings, "The unexamined life is not worth living" and "Know thyself." The Socratic ethic was a philosophy of self-fulfillment through increasing knowledge of the self. The steadfast determination of his own moral character included his resistance and refusal to obey what he deemed the unjust laws of the Athenian government. In effect, he was then executed at the foolish whim of the city officials, which was a clear object lesson to his followers regarding the wise man versus the state. Antisthenes, student and companion of

Socrates, would draw the conclusion that the law of individual virtue and the laws of the established state were natural enemies. When Diogenes came to Athens, he soon fell into the company of Antisthenes, still reeling from the execution of his friend Socrates. Diogenes thus took up the cudgels against the follies and vagaries of established conventions in the living out of his own unique mission to the world.

It is said that wherever he went and whatever he did he constantly attempted to shock his fellows into the realization that the development of oneself requires the casting off of social conventions, which are no more than the fetters of individual realization. For this reason, Diogenes behaved in the most outrageous and unconventional manner. He and his school took the name of "Cynic," which is the Greek word for "dog," and clearly indicates a desire to distinguish himself from both the common people and the upper classes. Diogenes was likewise in the habit of dressing in the very shabbiest of garb and begging for his daily sustenance. It is reported by Laertius that Alexander the Great once came to him and stated, "I am Alexander the Great," to which Diogenes replied, "I am Diogenes the Dog." When Alexander asked him what he had done to be called a dog, Diogenes retorted, "I fawn on those who give me anything, I yelp at those who refuse, and I set my teeth in rascals."[3] It is not clear whether Diogenes actually set his teeth in the "Great One," but when Alexander amusedly asked what he might do for him, Diogenes composedly replied, "Stand out of my light," which must have been quite a put-down to the most powerful man in the world. Despite the insult, however, Alexander was quite obviously impressed with the complete individuality of the Dog, for he is reported to have said, "Had I not been Alexander, I should have liked to be Diogenes."[4]

Laertius also reports that one day at a feast, the revelers kept throwing all the bones and scraps to Diogenes, as if to a dog. Diogenes, in turn, played the dog's trick and urinated all over the revelers. This likewise bespeaks an unusual talent, especially if we are to accept the wording of Laertius who states that Diogenes actually "drenched" them.[5]

Upon coming to Athens, Diogenes had difficulty finding suitable lodgings, and we might guess that many landlords would not have been overly enthusiastic about renting to him. Undaunted, Diogenes simply took up residence in an old tub in the public square, and he continued to live there throughout his life, which stretched for some ninety years. As Laertius noted, "It was his habit to do everything in public, including the works of Demeter and Aphrodite alike."[6] Laertius is here employing a euphemism which means that Diogenes did as he damned well pleased. Aphrodite, for example, was the goddess of love, and Diogenes was in the habit of performing her works in public. Roughly translated, Diogenes was given to masturbation and copulation in full view of the citizenry!

Traveling the city of Athens in the clothes of a beggar, renouncing all property, going about with half his head shaven and the other half sporting a full growth, Diogenes would take full opportunity to display his own offbeat ways in order to prick the conventional conscience of his fellows. Observing the political and economic ambitions of the citizenry, Diogenes lit a lamp in broad daylight and went about the city proclaiming that he was looking for the honest man.[7] Nothing was too outrageous for him, and his only goal was to achieve complete freedom from what he believed to be the artificiality of custom and accepted beliefs.

By the account of Laertius, Diogenes was truly a master of wit and the clever saying, and he was not at all bashful about rendering his fellows come-uppant. At the same time, however, he was far from hostile but rather tended to employ his gift with words as a means of producing insight into the behavior of others. Once on a voyage, he was captured by pirates and taken to Crete, where he was to be sold into slavery. When the auctioneer asked him in what he was proficient, Diogenes replied, "In governing men." He then picked out a sheepish-looking man in the crowd and said, "Sell me to this man; he needs a master." The man, one Xeniades, then bought him and made Diogenes the teacher of his children.[8]

Diogenes was stringently opposed to all the blind customs of his day, including the accepted practice of homosexuality among boys. When an effeminately attired youth once asked a question of him, Diogenes refused to answer unless the youth pulled up his robe to show whether he was a man or a woman.[9] To another overbearing young man who was complaining that so many people annoyed him with their attentions, Diogenes advised, "Cease to hang out a sign of invitation."[10] When he saw a boy, known to be the son of a courtesan, disdainfully throwing stones at a crowd, Diogenes chided, "Take care that you don't hit your father."[11]

From the brief descriptions of Laertius, it is clear that Diogenes frequently encountered the leading philosophers, such as Plato, in public discussion and regularly bested them, sometimes exposing their vain deceits. Plato, for example, had defined Man as a featherless biped, and he was roundly applauded for his cleverness. Diogenes plucked a fowl and brought it into the lecture room, with the words, "Here is Plato's man."[12] Diogenes was obviously not especially endeared to Plato. Thus, Plato one day saw him washing lettuces in the public square and chided him, "Had you paid homage to the gods, you wouldn't now be washing lettuces." With equal calmness, Diogenes pointed out, "If you had washed lettuces, you wouldn't have paid homage to the gods."[13]

The life of Diogenes was spent in the living of his philosophy. When someone declared that life itself was evil, Diogenes countered that the evil was not in life itself but rather in living poorly.[14] To Diogenes, of course, living well meant living out the life of the philosopher. When someone protested that they were not well adapted to the study of philosophy, he asked, "Why then do you live, if you do not care to live well?"[15] One day, someone asked him why people give money to beggars but not to philosophers, and he replied, "Because they think they may one day be lame or blind, but never expect that they will turn to philosophy."[16] For Diogenes, philosophy was no more and no less than the living pursuit and experience of a life that was free from convention and social custom. The wisdom was in the living and not merely in the saying. His friend Hegesias once asked Diogenes for the loan of some of his writings, and the Dog replied, "You are a simpleton, Hegesias; you do not choose painted figs, but real ones; and yet you pass over the true training and would apply yourself to written rules."[17] His actual behavior was intended, by force of his reasoning, to be much more meaningful than anything that he could write on paper.

It is fitting, therefore, that he has left posterity little more than the account of Laertius regarding his amazingly unconventional and unique way of life. His writings are all lost, and yet the impact of his life, to both peers and posterity, is not in his words but in his behavior. It is said that, at his death, all Athens mourned because he was so loved. On his grave, the following verse was inscribed:

> Time makes even bronze grow old: but thy glory, Diogenes, all eternity will never destroy. Since thou alone didst point out to mortals the lesson of self-sufficingness and the easiest path to life.[18]

In his later years, Diogenes would typically respond to questions about his origin and native city with the statement, "I am a citizen of the world."[19] He did not consider himself bound by the local customs, and as Laertius puts it, "he used any place for any purpose, for breakfasting, sleeping and conversing."[20] In this, he held firmly to the very last. When Xeniades asked him, very late in his life, how he wished to be buried, he replied, "On my face!" and to the quizzical "Why?"

of Xeniades he explained, "Because after a little time down will be converted to up."[21] His immense sensitivity to the vagaries of custom and the relativity of convention required him to be true only to himself, expressing allegiance to no one other than his own spirit. In this respect, Diogenes was truly the most cosmopolitan of oddballs, and we must wonder at the deeper lessons and more profound meaning of his immensely unusual life.

For Diogenes, the overriding and indeed consuming obligation of the free man was to become wise, to live the life of wisdom. Laertius sums up the teachings of Diogenes quite simply:

> He maintained that all things are the property of the wise, and employed such arguments as those cited above. All things belong to the gods. The gods are friends to the wise, and friends share all property in common; therefore all things are the property of the wise. Again as to law, that it is impossible for society to exist without law; for without a city no benefit can be derived from that which is civilized. But the city is civilized, and there is no advantage in law without a city; therefore law is something civilized. He would ridicule good birth and fame and all such distinctions, calling them showy ornaments of vice. The only true commonwealth was, he said, that which is as wide as the universe.[22]

In its essentials, Diogenes presents a simple message that separates the wheat from the chaff. In so many ways, he maintains that civilization has a tendency to complicate the utter simplicity of life, that the force of customs and conventions is to narrow one's scope and fog one's vision. To Diogenes, the ultimate sense and meaning of any belief and/or behavior is its test at the bar of reason, the practical reason of the wise man who will seek the virtuous act and render the intelligent judgment. The gist of the Cynic approach, of which Diogenes was the most bold and original proponent, was that the meaning of virtue could not be found merely in the laws and customs of civilized society but rather in the searching out of oneself.

J. M. Rist, in his excellent review of Cynic philosophy, raises the central question in Cynicism as a philosophy. It is worth, I think, quoting him in complete context.

> The principal difficulty in our understanding of Cynicism is to know what virtuous acts are. Again and again we find accounts of what the wise man will not be concerned with, the sham values of everyday life; but it is difficult to find any account of a course of action which is positively good. Doubtless the Cynics claimed that it is good to be completely independent of one's society, but what are the acts of a completely independent man?
>
> Diogenes himself claimed that freedom of speech and freedom of action are the most important things in life. This freedom has been interpreted . . . as freedom from all restraint whatsoever; that is an understandable, but slightly misleading explanation. It is probably true that Diogenes thought that the wise man could say almost anything, and that he could (and would) do all kinds of things which the conventional public (the fools) would feel inhibited about. But clearly, however much he exaggerated his utterances about freedom, Diogenes would not have the wise man say that vice is good, even though he is perfectly free to say that public masturbation, for example, is totally indifferent morally. Diogenes is not an amoralist. . . The freedom of his wise man is a freedom to act in accordance with what is right and to say what is right, regardless of any other considerations than his own judgment. Yet it is easy to see why Diogenes looks like an amoralist, indeed why for the same reasons he was called a "dog" in antiquity. It is because he continually explained what is not vicious, because natural, while never giving details about what is virtuous. It might be argued that his real opinion was that virtue is simply the complete independence of the

self; but even that would probably not be a full description of what Diogenes intended, for he seems to have thought that the completely independent man would act *qua* independent man in certain specific ways in particular situations. . . . Diogenes tells us that all our actions must be governed by virtue, by a recognition of what is good, but he does not tell us what virtue is.[23]

Rist, a respectable philosopher and historian of philosophy, rightly underlines the fact that Diogenes is not a madman, either psychologically or ethically speaking. The oddball antics of Diogenes constitute meaningful events in the history of human endeavor and are worthy of thoughtful consideration by other wise men. Rist also indicates, however, his own difficulty in sorting out the complex subtleties of a genuinely oddball position, which at its heart is awesomely simple. In effect, he asks Diogenes to give a list of rules about the nature of the virtuous act and the virtuous life. He asks Diogenes to translate himself into a set of social conventions! Diogenes is required by Rist to spell it out in the very way that he abhorred it in others. The frightening implication of the life of Diogenes, of course, is the underlying question of whether any man can discover "right and good" for any other man, or whether we are, all of us, in both the long run and the short run, left to our own determination of what is right and good for each of us. To me, Diogenes clearly and assuredly intends to demonstrate that human life cannot be reduced to a set of social conventions but that it can be reduced to an inner sense of direction and a realization of the unique meaning of one's own life. And to a large degree, this inner meaning may well be incommunicable, except as it might be inferred by the unique behavior of the person in question. To the extent that one infers in another only the common characteristics of convention and custom, then one has not really touched upon the right, the good, and the true, let alone the dynamic reality of the individual.

It was inevitable, of course, that Diogenes the Dog would be effective in his life and teaching, that he would

acquire followers, that soon Cynicism would become a movement with its own conventions and ideals, and inevitably its
own self-fulfilling destiny, another commonalized form of
human experience. The brilliant Theodor Gomperz, in his
monumental history of Greek philosophy, traces with typical
vigor the conventionalization of the heritage of oddball
Diogenes into a veritable society of philosopher-dogs who
lived in their tubs.

> The resistance of an inert world soon convinced the
> Cynic, if he had not known it from the first, that his
> ideals stood little chance of realization within the pale of
> existing institutions. He therefore did his utmost to place
> his own person outside the circle of social life. He
> renounced all the cares of property; he formed no family
> ties; he abode in no settled dwelling-place. Not only did
> he hold aloof from politics, but, in his capacity of "world-
> citizen," he viewed with indifference the fortunes of his
> own city and nation. He chose the life of a beggar. His
> long, shaggy hair and beard, his wallet or beggar's
> pouch, his staff, his cloak of coarse cloth—the only
> covering he wore winter or summer—these were the
> outward tokens of his sect, the marks which sometimes
> procured him honour, but more often contempt and
> even blows. . . .
>
> All the motives that govern the life of the average
> man, particularly the craving for wealth and power, all
> the ideals to which the common herd look up in re-
> spectful admiration, passed with the Cynics for "illu-
> sion." "Freedom from illusion" was their motto. . . . An
> insatiable thirst for freedom, a profound sensitiveness to
> the ills of life, an unshakeable faith in the majesty and all-
> sufficiency of reason, and a corresponding abysmal
> contempt for all traditional ideals, —such are the moods
> and the convictions which lie at the root of
> Cynicism. . . .[24]

Thus, in time, the bold, creative individuality of Diogenes was reduced to a pattern of Cynic conventions and

beliefs, still at odds with the larger society, but nonetheless dedicated to an increasing set of customs within their philosopher-dogs group. They were no longer citizens of the world in the sense that Diogenes was, in the sense of a seeker of experience as wide as the universe. They had become citizens of the school of Cynicism, holders of the Cynic conventions, and proponents of the Cynic world-view. Would Diogenes have approved the fruits of his legacy or would he have turned face down again in his grave?

An army of Cynic beggars roaming the countrysides and cities of an ancient Greece and Rome, repeating the acts of the founder, mouthing the sayings of a long-gone oddball would, of course, have been as ridiculous to Diogenes as any of the other forms of conventionalized behavior. They would have been to Diogenes a failure of wisdom, a derogation of self-realization, a mockery of individual freedom. A society of unconventionalists is a contradiction of terms and reality, and Diogenes constantly attempted to point out the power of convention and social pressure in destroying inward peace. The life of Diogenes was not a game of "can-I-be-more-outrageous-than-you?", or, worse yet, "how-well-can-I-copy-you-in-being-outrageous?" His flagrant deeds were constantly intended to demonstrate the conscious or unconscious sources of social influence controlling or at least competing with the individual's ability to govern himself. The invitation of Diogenes "to be and do like me" was not a call to imitate his deed or words but rather a call to become wise in one's own way, whatever course one's inner direction might provide. He would have been shocked at the witness of an army of imitators, dressing, acting, and talking as he did.

Historians often look upon Diogenes as one of the first in a long succession of radical (and unsuccessful) social reformers. I believe this to be an error in understanding, for Diogenes is much more an individual reformer than a mere bum-rapper of social institutions. He requires a man to look at himself and to place his own rules of conduct under the tough scrutiny of reason and good sense. Why do we behave as we do? Why do we think as we do? Why do we exist as we are? These are the issues that Diogenes stirs in the individual consciousness of anyone able to hear. Am I able to claim my life as my own?

The Diogenian contempt for social institutions and the public morals that derive therefrom is no more than the Socratic concern for the individual unexamined life. And as Socrates said, such is not worth living. To both the simple city-state of ancient Greece as well as to the complex megalopolis of the contemporary world, Diogenes is a freak. In a modern society, which regularly presents the sterile image of the faceless multitudes that haunt the jammed expressways each dawn and dusk, the message of Diogenes is especially frightening. He asks us to be ourselves. And how are we to find the roots of individuation in the maze of constant stop-and-go traffic?

6 The Prophet Ezekiel

Visions, Rituals, and Symbolic Oddballitry

THERE IS A saying that has long been extant in Israel: "Where there is no vision, the people perish." Israel, more than any other people or nation, has been especially sensitive and receptive to the man of vision, and the early history of the Jews is particularly fraught with the emergence of the unusual man at a time of crisis. When the Egyptians were literally killing off the Hebrews in the service of their own civilization, Moses came out of the bullrushes to lead his people out of Egypt and to provide them with a sense of destiny. At the death of Moses, young, dynamic Josue came to the fore, receiving the promise of the Lord to settle the people in the land of Canaan. Half a millennium later, the Assyrians, first under Tiglath-pileser and then under Sennacherib, begin a succession of assaults and victories against the nation of Israel, and the men of vision came in earnest, undisguised as the prophets of the Lord. In the footsteps of Elijah and Elisha came Amos, Hosea, Isaiah, Micah, Jeremiah, a steady stream of prophetic visionaries raised up by the Lord to dream a dream and see a vision, so that the people would not perish.

Much of the Old Testament literature is, of course, the very story and teaching of the prophets of Israel. An odd lot, indeed, the prophets are, and the modern reader, no matter what his religious persuasion or lack thereof, is hard put not to sense their ecstatic vision and state of spiritual exaltation. Each of the prophets, in his own way, testifies to an experience of union with a force larger than himself, with God, which led him to a consciousness of self as an instrument of the Lord. Each of them testifies to the experience of a genuine vision, not just an intellectualized view, but a genuine vision. As one Biblical scholar has ventured:

> In this condition the prophet ceased to be aware of the ordinary circumstances and relationships of life and became intensely aware of God. The personality of the prophet was not set aside; it was raised to a new intensity through encounter with God, and became the medium of divine revelation.[1]

There would be no purpose here in repeating the many-sided debates about the nature and reality of prophecy and the prophets; nonetheless, within the limits of this study there is cause for interest in this issue of intensified personalization, believed to be a characteristic of the prophet. In my own recent reading of the prophetic books, it is likewise clear to me that the failure to include a representative prophet or two in a book on oddballs would be a serious oversight. The prophets are indeed a very kooky group. The contemporary believer often assumes that the religious leaders depicted in the Bible must have been cut from the same cloth as Billy Graham or Pope Pius XII or similar pillars of established religion. Even a casual reading of the Biblical texts, however, will easily indicate that the prophets were more akin to the classic curmudgeon than to the modern models of genteel sociality who man the current religious establishment. The prophets did some really weird deeds. The Book of Isaiah, for example, mentions some unconventional activity on the part of the prophet:

The Lord gave a warning through Isaiah, the son of Amos: Go and take off the sackcloth from your waist, and remove the sandals from your feet. This he did, walking naked and barefoot. Then the Lord said: Just as my servant Isaiah has gone naked and barefoot for three years as a sign and portent against Egypt and Ethiopia, so shall the king of Assyria lead away captives from Egypt, and exiles from Ethiopia, young and old, naked and barefoot, with buttocks uncovered (the shame of Egypt). (Isaiah, 20:2-4)

What was Isaiah doing in that sackcloth in the first place, let alone taking it off for three years in an *au naturel* parade before the Israelites, Egyptians, and Ethiopians? And if the Egyptians would be ashamed about their uncovered buttocks, wouldn't Isaiah, if he were on the side of the normals, tend to blush a bit about his own bare *derriere*? How straight could old Isaiah have been? Three years of x-rated behavior must have done wonders for his own sense of intensified personalization!

Each of the prophets engaged in sufficiently strange antics that many moderns are inclined to see them as a group of lunatics. With the advent of the psychiatric movement in our contemporary culture, there is a prevailing tendency to diagnose "strange" people as manifesting a particular form of psychopathology. Yet much of the behavior and the experience of the prophets could easily be viewed and understood in the professional psychiatric jargon of a state mental institution. Abraham Heschel, in his well-regarded study of the prophets, has a lengthy chapter on the pros and cons of "Prophecy and Psychosis." Heschel's examination of the psychiatric opinions and psychological analyses of the prophetic personality comes to the following conclusion:

> It is not for any psychological analysis, nor for any socio-logical or anthropological reasoning, however profound and imaginative, however patient and exact, to have the last word about the nature of prophecy. Such analysis or reasoning is prone to reduce prophecy to a common-

place too irrelevant to justify the effort of analysis. And yet the phenomenon of the prophets continues to remain provocative, alarmingly relevant, despite its incomprehensibility.[2]

I am inclined to agree with Heschel, without necessarily sharing his religious convictions. There is no need to treat religious realities as though they were merely psychological realities, easily explained away by current theories of human functioning and malfunctioning. Instead of debunking the beliefs of organized religion, I find myself quite awed by the highly unusual and individualized behavior spelled out in the various books of the prophets. At the same time, there is no need to discount the testimony of the Biblical literature itself that the prophets were often seen as madmen by their own contemporaries (cf. Jeremiah, 29:26). From the standpoint of this investigation, we are interested in the dynamically individualized person, whatever his particular claim to fame, and the writings of the prophets present much food for thought on the oddball as oddball.

Among the prophets there is one who stands out as even more provocative and incomprehensible than the norm for prophets themselves. Ezekiel, who began his prophetic ministry shortly after Babylonia conquered Jerusalem and brought the Jews to Babylon in exile (598 B.C.), is a marvelously weird character, given to very puzzling behavior and exceedingly strange visions. As the Catholic Biblicist Joseph Grispino notes,

Ezechiel's personality is one of contrasts; he is the most challenging Old Testament prophet to understand as a person. It is relevant to note here the prohibition of the rabbis in St. Jerome's time which barred the reading of Ezechiel's visions until the age of thirty. Ezechiel's character easily arouses interest. He is a priest who preaches ("prophet") and writes. His message is half on the destruction of the people and half on their restoration to happiness. His cast of mind seems that of a visionary as well as that of a realist.[3]

Any genuine prophet who can make it to the Jewish index of forbidden books merits serious consideration from the vantage of oddballitry.

I had long been a member of the over-thirty crowd when I first stumbled on the visions of Ezekiel, and I can well understand the prohibition of the rabbis. Some of his stuff is farther out than anyone who has ever tripped on mescaline or LSD. The opening vision of the book of Ezekiel is a huge cloud of flashing fire enveloping four very squirrelly figures, each of them with four faces and four wings and sparkling with the gleam of burnished bronze. The four-sided faces included that of a man, a lion, an ox, and an eagle, and later writers have seen here a prophecy of the four evangelists of the New Testament. Each of the creatures had swooping wings and moved about on whirling wheels of sparkling chrysolite, which moved as one with the creatures themselves. The roar of their wings was like the voice of the Almighty amidst the tumultuous din of an army, and it was in the vision itself that the Lord spoke to Ezekiel, commanding him to eat a scroll. To eat a scroll?

Ezekiel was not only given to seeing very strange goings-on; he was also given to committing some very strange goings-on, of which the eating of a scroll is not the least example. In the midst of his opening vision of the Lord descending upon him, Ezekiel relates the following:

> It was then that I saw a hand stretch out to me, in which was a written scroll which he unrolled before me. It was covered with writing front and back, and written on it was: Lamentation and wailing and woe!
> He said to me: Son of man, eat what is before you; eat this scroll, then go, speak to the house of Israel. So I opened my mouth and he gave me the scroll to eat. Son of man, he then said to me, feed your belly and fill your stomach with this scroll I am giving you. I ate it, and it was as sweet as honey in my mouth. He said: Son of man, go now to the house of Israel, and speak my words to them. (Ezekiel, 2:9-3:4)

Commentators on the book of Ezekiel tell us that the eating of the scroll was a form of symbolic behavior, but the commentators are inclined to interpret all of the zany antics of the prophets as symbols of some deeper religious meaning. In the inner sanctums of the psychiatric establishment, such behavior is commonly referred to as paranoid schizophrenia, actively delusional, in which case the practitioner of said behavior and vision is usually referred to some asylum or another for lengthy bedrest. In other words, the current practice is to treat such strange behavior as psychotic and to refer the individual to psychiatric help. In Old Testament times, however, these manifestations of weirdness were seen as the calling cards of prophecy, and the populace was inclined to await the development of the prophetic manifestation. There is a message here, I believe, about the relativity of conventions as well as the respective tolerance for and interpretation of dynamic oddballitry as practiced by various social groups in different historical epochs and cultures. To the "house of Israel" the antics of Ezekiel were received as a message from God rather than just some freak doing his thing. Whatever the possible differences that might exist between various social groups, however, Ezekiel's vision, which culminates in the mastication and digestion of the scroll (real or hallucinated), is unquestionably an example of highly individuated behavior. My point is that Ezekiel serves as an example of dynamic oddballitry that rises above all known social settings and formats of collective convention (with the exception of the asylum as previously noted).

This intensified personalization of Ezekiel is understood by the believer as the Spirit of the Lord taking hold of him. Whatever the dynamics of his individualization, Ezekiel continued in his program of strange visions and outrageous behavior. Chapter 4 of the Book of Ezekiel relates how he built a model of the city of Jerusalem from clay bricks and proceeded to act out a pretend attack on his toy city; this he did not in the privacy of his own bedroom but rather in full view of his colleagues. The commentators state that this behavior is symbolic and prophetic of God's intent to over-throw the city. It certainly is an unusual device for God as well as a grown man.

In the same chapter, Ezekiel describes the time that he lay down on his left side for 390 days and then on his right side for 40 more days. This would be a considerable feat for even the most accomplished catatonic, let alone for someone who is given to such active visions. We are told, again, that this behavior was in response to Ezekiel's experience of God's direction, and that these days of "lying fallow" were literally symbolic of the captivity of Israel and the captivity of Judah. Because this feat was accomplished in pre-Olympic days, Ezekiel has never been credited with a world record in this regard. There can be no doubt, however, that Ezekiel was responsible for one of the more enduring spectacles in the history of Babylon, which was noted even in ancient times for some fairly steamy events.

On another occasion, Ezekiel cut off the hair of his head and beard with a sword sharpened to the cut of a barber's razor. He then divided his shorn hair into three parts. He burned the first part. The second part, he struck with a sword. He then took the last third of his shorn hair and scattered it to the winds. The commentators here see the prophecy of the fate of the people of Israel: "These actions depicted the fate of the people of Jerusalem; many would die of disease and famine, some would be slain, others would be scattered in exile."[4]

Ezekiel is responsible for a variety of egregious actions, but rather than being ostracized as a weirdo he is canonized as a prophet. It is, I guess, a simple datum of the human mystery that some freaks are false prophets whereas others become institutionalized as idols of the common man. The freakishness of Ezekiel is an example of oddball behavior that is eventually extolled as the highest form of personalization, the union of a man with God. Contemporary commentators maintain that it is the very outrageousness of his behavior that bespeaks God's action and intervention. Ezekiel's outlandish stunts are praised for their shock value in that they call attention, symbolically it is said, to the larger issue of God's loving concern for mankind. Biblical scholars to a man will argue the case for the latent meaning of Ezekiel's outlandish antics, finding here dramatic proof of God's intervention in human affairs. As Winward maintains:

> "Actions speak louder than words." By means of these dramatic demonstrations, engaging the eyes as well as the ears of the people, the message of God was driven home. That which the prophet had proclaimed in words was expressed and embodied in actions. It would be a mistake, however, to regard these symbolic acts as little more than "visual aids" to a deeper understanding of the truth. "Like the spoken word, they are instrumental acts, helping to bring about that which they signify. They are part of the divine activity, that part which the prophets initiate." [Quoting H. Wheeler-Robinson, *Redemption and Revelation*, p. 250]
> . . . They convey the unseen realities they symbolize, even though they symbolize far more than they convey. Through them God acts here and now; yet they also point forward to his action in the future. God was acting through the symbolic acts of Ezekiel and yet those acts themselves pointed to the greater action of God in history, in which they were fulfilled.[5]

According to the commentators, then, the more outrageous the prophet's behavior, the more apparent is the unseen intervention of God. While some oddballs are forgotten or condemned to obscurity, others achieve stunning heights of human esteem and their respective pieces of weirdness serve future generations as beacons searching the heavens for intimations of divinity.

It is likewise true that the book of Ezekiel has endured these many generations for reasons other than the prophet's goofy behavior. The overall quality of his theology testifies that he was more than just a freak on the loose. If one reads the whole of Ezekiel and stumbles through the initial hallucinogenic atmosphere of visions gone wild in the service of some fairly aberrant behavior, one also becomes aware that Ezekiel is a man of considerable intellectual attainment. He trains the reader in a fairly creative understanding of man's moral activity and sense of responsibility. Eventually, Ezekiel gets down to the brass tacks of preaching a very basic message of human accountability and personal responsibility for one's own life and one's own actions. By the end of his book, Ezekiel is "all priest," laying out the codes and rituals of righteousness in a dollars-and-cents fashion.

The latter chapters of the book of Ezekiel read like a basic catechism of religious ceremonial and ritualistic convention. The fundamentals of Hebraic worship are spelled out with magnificent simplicity, so that it becomes impossible for the practitioner to mistake the full gravity of his obligation to behave in a religiously acceptable fashion. The schizophrenic-like hallucinations of the early chapters gradually fall into the regular cadence of obsessive-compulsive simplicity; the early madman becomes the great conventionalist. The heights of symbolic creativity have been scaled, and the highly personalized oddball becomes the codifier of religious practice.

As Edith Hamilton has opined, "Ezekiel is the first religious organizer we know about and the greatest."[6] The incredible temerity of Ezekiel the Visionary would find its real fruition in the establishment, once and for all, of fundamental Hebraic religion which remains unchanged since the time that Ezekiel made his pronouncements and reform of circumcision, dietary laws, and ritualistic worship. Hamilton has gone right to the nub of it:

With all of his dreams and visions he was exceedingly practical. The combination is not as unusual as it may seem at first sight, and it results in a tremendously effective personality, one with the absolute certainty that takes possession of a man convinced that he has actually seen the truth, and at the same time with the ability to make the truth work efficiently. St. Paul was like that and so was St. Augustine. Luther is an example too and Mahomet supremely so. These men were triumphantly successful organizers. But Ezechiel was the forerunner and his methods were followed, consciously or unconsciously, by them all. He is the model organizer of religion.[7]

As one scratches at the roots of the most organized, most conventional, most prosaic of enterprises, one finds there the footprints of the oddball. The cultic practices of occidental religion are found to have their origin in the catatonic who lay on his left side for 390 days, give or take a few minutes. The common rituals of the many are traced back to the outrageous individuality of the one. In the aftermath of his earlier visions and offbeat antics at the prompting of the Lord, Ezekiel settled down to the basic business of religious reform, of getting people to behave his way, or at least having them conform to the dictates of the God who spoke through him. In the long run, Ezekiel screwed every man to his sticking place, third aisle/middle pew and eager to drop his shekels at the passing of the plate. Ezekiel the prophet became Ezekiel the religious organizer; and yet, behind the most finely honed customs and mores of organized religion, still there lurks the unseemly shenanigans of the oddball.

We began this chapter with an old Jewish saying, "Where there is no vision, the people perish." In the vision of Ezekiel, there was room for both the outrageous act as well as for the commonplace behavior. Ezekiel bridged the gap between the spasms of personalized individuality and the daily exigencies of the social group. He was a many-sided man, a man of many moods and various sensibilities. His was the singular thrust of the man aflame as well as the plodding movement of the organizer and the stabilizer. His splash of individuality left a wake of organized rituals and practices, and consciously so. He moved as easily from the flights of individual fantasy to the basic statement of required behavior for the many. Perhaps he was a man compelled by God to feel that which he felt. Perhaps this was why he settled so many compulsive requirements on the historical religion of the West. From the psychedelic sense of his own conscious-ness of God, he came to found the highly ritualized conven-tions of the synagogue. And yet, this "father of Judaism," as he is commonly known, began the whole bailiwick of organ-ized religion by chewing on an imaginary scroll.

Like Diogenes, Ezekiel acted oddly for good reason. Like Diogenes, his reason for the flagrant deed was to have others examine the bases of their own behavior. Like Dio-genes, his behavior was intended to service a higher ideal; where Diogenes sought the wisdom of philosophic reason, Ezekiel felt himself to be the messenger of God. Unlike Diogenes, he sensed he stood for something larger than himself. Therefore, he came to preach religion for the many and searched to find a way by which the many could find contact with that transcendent something he had found within himself.

In the past 2,500 years, generation upon generation has acted out the solemn rituals of that self-same cultic ob-servance fashioned at the hands of Ezekiel. Jew and Chris-tian alike have found a comfortable home in the repetitious service of synagogue and church. The organized religions of the Western world have found their glue and basic structure in the codes set forth by the father of Judaism. And yet, to me, he will always be the man who ate the scroll.

7 Jerry Rubin
Absurdity in Action

IN THE JUDGMENT of future generations, the 1960s in the United States of America will likely be seen as a decade of immense political upheaval and intense social change. For those who survived, it was a time when established political and social institutions were challenged and questioned with incredible vigor and regularly subjected to the most calloused invective. A time of shifting values and ambiguous standards, criticism and dissent were keystone activities, and the storming of one Bastille or another was an almost daily event.

Immense social unrest from divergent segments of society created strange bedfellows, united in a revolutionary spirit, though committed to differing goals and philosophies. This melting pot of dissatisfied people produced an explosive mixture of action and reaction, of revolutionary and reactionary, and the forces of change met again and again in heated and often violent confrontation with the protectors of the public trust. The riots at Berkeley, May Day at Yale, the People's March on Washington, the Columbia revolt, the Days of Rage, the 1968 Democratic Convention in Chicago, the tragedy of Kent State—these were but a few, and

73

perhaps more notorious, of the many encounters and conflicts between established, sanctioned authority and, to use Bayard Rustin's phrase, "the disaffected sons and daughters of the middle class."

The revolutionary spirit of the sixties was especially remarkable because the members of the movement were neither the downtrodden and the dispossessed nor the army of cranks and crackpots who are always ready and eager to well up against the established order. The movement was primarily composed of the sons and daughters and the brothers and the sisters of the abstract common man and common woman. This was a revolution in the midst of plenty, and the sociologists, psychologists, and professional analysts scurried back to their textbooks—if they had been able to save them from the local campus riot—in hurried attempts to find sensible explanations for such confusing realities. There have always been radicals of one persuasion or another to shoulder the blame for the conventional misadventure, but how could one explain the New Left, the SDS, Weatherman, hippies, flower children, the politics of despair, communes, counterculture, Yippies, NOW, Women's Lib, and the whole host of antiestablishment labels and realities?

Erik Erikson, a very abstruse psychoanalyst, became popular and it became customary for professors to talk about their own "identity crisis" as well as that of their students. In some fairly heavy theorizing, Erikson had advanced the notion of "negative identity" as a means by which the young achieve some semblance of a sense of self. It was said, then, that the young were identifying with everything that their parents were not and that the movement was the natural sociological extension of an underlying and fundamental psychological process. This theory found considerable credence in the emergence of the "antihero," and Charlie Chaplin became more popular than John Wayne. Armies of young men sprung up looking very much like a bumbling Elliot Gould in blue jeans and bandanna. A typical high school classroom looked like a contest in which all the young maidens were vying with each other to see whose hair could look as frizzied and unkempt as Janis Joplin's. In such an age, the guy with the briefcase and the pinstripe suit tended to look more like an oddball than anybody else, and it seemed as though a whole new generation of unconventionalists had sprung up.

Closer examination, of course, would simply reveal the emergence of new patterns of conformity and the development of a different set of social conventions. There is simply something about human nature that takes comfort in sameness, sociality, consciousness of kind, contact with others of a like nature and orientation, security, predictability, and the whole bag of an established social order. The 1970s are now half spent, and one can sense that the movement has slowed to a snail's pace, if not a crashing halt. Young people are scurrying back to law school and to business college and are concerned about jobs and getting ahead, much in the manner of their forebears. People are actually getting married again, instead of just living together. Alternate life-style is still very much in the air, although in many ways the notion itself has the earmarks of another packaged program. Social analysts again feel comfortable and knowledgeable and safely in control of their own intellects; new textbooks incorporate the experience of the sixties and are well armed with an entire antiestablishment typology and theory of change.

All of this would overlook the fact that within the revolutions of the sixties, there were some, perhaps many, who achieved new heights of individuality. The leaders of the movement—the Eldridge Cleavers, the Bernadine Dohrns, the Tom Haydens, the Bobby Seales, the Abbie Hoffmans, and so on—can take real solace in the knowledge that the focus of the political trial has shifted from the Chicago Conspiracy to the President of the United States and his henchmen. The wild and woolly antics of the sixties did not go for naught, neither in terms of a program for social change nor in terms of the sometime achievement of a highly refined sense of individuation. It is again the achievement of the oddball that is our main interest, but it is worth noting that some genuine oddballs were very much at the fore of productive social change within our own times.

It will be recalled that the behavior of both Diogenes and Ezekiel was designed to capture the attention of others in order to make known their own peculiar message. The outlandish stunt is obviously an old trick, probably practiced by the oddball since time immemorial. The egregious act is a shill, a come-on, an inducement, an entrapment, a threat or what-have-you by which the actor gains access to his audience in order to advertise his own platform. In the turmoil of the sixties, with its changing perspectives and topsy-turvy values, there were legions of weirdoes who took to the streets to do their own thing, but none were as charismatic, as genuinely primitive, as gifted with a knack for nuttiness, as eager to display themselves in public spectacle, as was Jerry Rubin. No slight is intended to the other dedicated freaks of the sixties, but Rubin is unquestionably the oddball nonpareil of the whole grubby lot.

Jerry Rubin is an object lesson in oddballitry. Never in his political scheming has he been damned by faint praise. His public personality was that of a loud, forceful, aggressive, mouthy intimidator who demands a gut-level response, always creating a variety of powerful emotions in his listeners and observers. In his heyday, he was a walking, talking, exhibitionistic sideshow of freaky stunts. At times he achieved new heights of profanity, and he always dedicated himself to the task of being as offensive and obnoxious as he could. In this, he has been as successful as any man could hope to be. Rubin could alienate entire governments in a single performance!

Rubin is of special interest to the study of oddballitry because he is also the author of a manual/autobiography on the basic dimensions and rationale of tripping to the funny farm. *Do It!* is a signal document because it is written by a convert, and converts are known for the intensity of their beliefs and the zeal of their commitment. In other words, Jerry Rubin was not always an oddball. He was born and raised in straight society, went to a good college, and worked as a sports reporter for a reputable Cincinnati newspaper, and throughout his early years was a convention-loving supporter of law and order.

And then, ZAP! Rubin was smitten. The dynamics of his conversion are shrouded in mystery, but the fact itself became progressively apparent during his graduate school days in the middle of the Berkeley uprisings. It would be a mistake to regard Rubin merely as another spouter of socialist rhetoric about "up with the people" and "down with the capitalist pigs." He does a lot of that, of course, and his own socialist, radical-left platform is singularly uninspiring. He is not a profound thinker, and his theoretical contributions to the movement and revolution in general are little more than claptrap jargon. Ah, but when it comes to pure oddballitry, he is unexcelled in his own time. Rubin's mastery of the dynamics of individuality is truly creative and has enabled him to achieve behavioral feats of unequaled distinction. In this respect, *Do It!* is a remarkable chronicle of his conscious attempt to explore the outer limits of outrageous behavior, all in the service of personal freedom.

In *Do It!*, Rubin lays out the basics of absurd behavior in the following fashion.

> The role of the revolutionary is to create theatre which creates a revolutionary frame of reference. The power to define is the power to control. . . . Fear and paranoia are the luxuries of the suburban leftists, armchair intellectuals, graduate students, the uninvolved. The further you are from the movement, the more scared you become. The Black Panthers aren't afraid. The yippies aren't afraid. The Viet Cong aren't afraid. But in your

living room, you're scared shitless. And that's just where the power structure wants you. In the middle of a riot, I've never found anybody who's chickenshit. The way to eliminate fear is to do what you're most afraid of. The goal of theatre is to get as many people as possible to overcome fear by taking action. We create reality wherever we go by living our phantasies.[1]

Within the context of this counterphobic dynamic, this attempt to achieve freedom from fear by rushing headlong toward its source, Rubin forms an intellectual basis for his own unique contribution to oddballitry, the theatre. In Rubinian dimensions, theatre is public oddballitry in action. The intent of theatre is to demonstrate the fundamental absurdity of the existing social order as well as the absurdity of any individual's allegiance to that order. In order to do so, one must create confrontations with the functionaries and leaders of the establishment. Such confrontations are achieved, of course, by being as absolutely ridiculous as possible. By engaging in displays of utter madness, one invites the contempt of the powers that be, thus exposing the existing order for its ruthless, corrupt, insensitive, mercenary self.

The theatre confrontation is an invitation to all parties. The forces of the social order are invited to expose themelves as they really are, namely, absolutely contemptible. Rubin and his cohorts in the movement are invited to expose themselves as they really are, absolutely crazy. The onlookers, the great "Amerikan" public, are invited to dynamize and activate their own sense of freedom from the absurdity of the social order, so that they can be free in and of themselves to create their own realities, as odd as such realities might be. With this underlying rationale, Rubin has sensed his license to do anything he damn well pleases and to do it, *Do It!*, with as much absurdity as possible. In this, he has been well-nigh inimitable, engaging admirably and regularly in fits and feats of oddball anarchy. His massive orchestrations of "theatre" have earned him the reputation as the P.T. Barnum of the revolution, but his own personal zaniness exceeds even his considerable talent to drive others zany.

Rubin's appearances in the mid and late 1960s before the House UnAmerican Activities Committee (HUAC) catalogue the gradual emergence of his magnificent aptitude for showmanship. When HUAC began tossing off court invitations to a number of Berkeley radicals, Rubin tells us he had a bad case of "subpoena's envy," until he got one of his own. Initially, many of the subpoenaed in the movement thought about refusing to testify and pleading instead the First Amendment right to dissent. Rubin was outraged at the prospect of losing his opportunity to strut his stuff. In his own words,

> I never found the American people too uptight about the First Amendment anyway. The average baseball and football fans of Amerika can't be bored with legalistic constitutional bullshit. We've got to be as exciting as the Mets.
>
> "HUAC has destroyed reputations overnight and forced people to lose their jobs," said one member of the Communist Party.
>
> Reputations? We had *no* reputations to lose. Jobs? We had *no* jobs to lose. How could HUAC hurt us? What names could they call us? Communists? Anarchists? Traitors? Motherfuckers? The worse the better. . . . HUAC is a state of mind. It's only as powerful as your paranoia. If you're scared of it, it's 100 feet tall. If you laugh at it the whole world laughs with you.
>
> What were HUAC members going to do when they found themselves face-to-face with the biggest media freaks and publicity seekers since Jesus Christ?
>
> I began thinking about HUAC as theater: I knew that I could not play on their stage, because they hold power in their gavel. I had to create my own theater to mindfuck HUAC and capture the nation's attention. But how?[2]

In this passage, the inner workings of Rubin's conscious

attempt to scale the heights of public outrageousness are displayed as a sense of exhibitionism with impunity. Rubin would, in fact, turn the HUAC hearings into a costume ball, himself appearing dressed perfectly in the garb of an "Amerikan" Revolutionary soldier, complete with tricornered hat, passing out parchment copies of the Declaration of Independence (purchased, by the way, from the John Birch Society). Although he did act outrageously enough to be charged with disorderly conduct, the hearings were called off before Rubin really had sufficient opportunity to be his utterly nutty self.

In September 1968, Rubin again achieved the distinction of HUAC subpoena. Another chance at unmitigated zaniness before the American public. Rubin decided to appear as a "one-man international revolution, a walking conspiracy."

> I arrived wearing a Black Panther beret with Panther and Yippie buttons, Egyptian earrings, a Mexican bandolier with live 303 British Infield bullets around my chest, black silk Viet Cong pajamas, jangling ankle bracelets, beads, and a headband. I had cowbells and jingle bells around my neck, wrists, and ankles so that every time I moved I sounded like an orchestra. My face, naked hairy chest and bare feet were painted with psychedelic designs and peace symbols. Over my shoulder I carried a toy M-16 custom-made rifle, the kind the Viet Cong use after stealing them from the Amerikans.[3]

The scene that followed was, of course, one of the more memorable moments in the halls of Congress, preserved for all posterity by every major newspaper in the country. Pictures of Rubin playing tug-of-war over his toy gun with uniformed police dotted the nation's wire services. It was finally agreed that Rubin could enter the Committee Room, but only if he disarmed himself of the real bullets! He was allowed to keep his toy M-16, which he used to great advantage, punctuating the meeting with shouts of "rat-a-tat-tat!" No one really worried though because all knew that he had been forced to leave his real bullets at the door. The absurdity of the establishment began to manifest itself, but just as Rubin was about to testify and really go into his act, Chairman Richard Ichord gaveled the meeting to a two-month recess.

When the committee reconvened, there was Jerry Rubin dressed as Santa Claus. Rubin, or Santa Claus, was barred from appearing, and the chairman ruled that before he would be called again to testify, he would have to undergo competent psychiatric examination. What would Rubin have to do to prove that he was nuts, and that oddball was better than normal? Being barred from Congress, however, was not for naught. A short month later, the House UnAmerican Activities Committee would propose to Congress a new law intended to outlaw insults to Congress through "cultural means." Rubin was absolutely exhilarated:

> What are cultural means? Dig it? Freaky clothes! *That's my law!* I wrote that law. I'm a legislator. Once upon a time congressmen could get laws through Congress. Now the average citizen can write laws. That should be everybody's goal. Write your own law. Do something so crazy that they got to pass new laws to outlaw it. They don't have enough laws now to stop what's going down. Make them *outlaw* you. Make yourself illegal![4]

Rubin's passion for individuality is so blatant that he would like to have a Congress of his own, committed to dealing only with his own behavior. His magnificent obsession with his narcissistic sense of self runs rampant at the prospect that the whole Congress might have to deal with a little piece of his whacked-out antics. Intellectually, of course, Rubin is opposed to all social and legal conventions—laws—as man-made enemies of the free, blithe spirit. Laws are the real obscenities, enslaving the people in workaday roles and attitudes. And yet, he just can't resist the wonderful absurdity of having a law passed purely for him. The anarchist is unearthed as taking sweet delight in laws of his own making.

Rubin, of course, was not opposed to all forms of

social organization. In company with Abbie Hoffman,[5] also an outstanding oddball, Rubin founded the Youth International Party, commonly known as the Yippies. He himself describes the Yippies as a "nonorganization, nonpolitical party," dedicated to a program of nonsense. "Its basic informational statement is a blank piece of paper," and its slogan is "Rise up and abandon the creeping meatball."[6] Many interpreted this perplexing platform as meaning that Rubin was a negativist, that he was against everything and in favor of nothing. At the Democratic National Convention of 1968, however, Rubin demonstrated that he was *for* something, that he did have a positive program. He and his party ran a pig, named Pigasus, for president of the United States. They attempted to declare his candidacy at the Picasso statue in Chicago's Civic Center, but everybody got arrested. They then demanded that Pigasus be flown to the Texas White House for foreign policy briefings, just like all the other presidential timber, but they just got busted all over again. The '68 convention in Chicago was extremely disappointing to Rubin, because each time he would come to the verge of something truly weird, he would get arrested.

The Yippie movement and *Do It!* are among Rubin's more efficacious attempts to corrupt the minds of youth and to teach them to rebel against the established social order and everything for which it stands. We will remember that Socrates was convicted by the city fathers of Athens on the very same charge. Although Rubin is a flesh-and-blood contemporary who is more offensive because of his very proximity, I fail to see any genuine differences between Rubin, on the one hand, and, say, Diogenes and Ezekiel, on the other. All are marvelously individualistic oddballs who use the outlandish public stunt as a means of calling people to a higher ethical ideal. Ezekiel's prophecy, Diogenes' cosmopolitanism, and Rubin's theatre are equally outrageous flights from and against the common and normative expectations of their respective peers and times. Each, in his own unique way, is genuinely anarchical and seeks to establish his own set of laws. Diogenes calls each man to shun the follies of conventional city life and to seek instead his own wisdom. Ezekiel calls each man away from the temptations of idolatry to seek personal righteousness in the worship of the one true God. Rubin calls each man to examine the travesty of a corrupting political order and to rise up against it by doing one's own thing. Diogenes, Ezekiel, and Rubin, I believe, share a common theme in being oddballs, that is, in being really different from a conventional view of how people are supposed to behave. In the same way, Moses, Darwin, and von Daniken share a striking similarity; despite the differences in their respective ideological systems, each developed a novel view in terms of the conventional ideas of his respective time.

Moses and Darwin, Diogenes and Ezekiel have all been rendered respectable by the passage of time. Darwin is the father of a highly regarded scientific theory. Diogenes is a classical Greek philosopher. Ezekiel is a real prophet, a Biblical authority and messenger from God. Moses is a symbol of a founding father. But they were all oddballs. Just as von Daniken and Rubin seem so goofy and foolish to this contemporary generation, so did Moses, Darwin, Ezekiel, and Diogenes seem genuinely nutty to their own peers. It is said that there is a thin line between genius and insanity, and not every oddball is a genius. But not everybody who dares to be different is insane either. It is difficult to tell whether von Daniken and Rubin, ideological and behavioral oddballs of our own era, will stand the test of time, whether they are sufficiently odd, sufficiently individualized, sufficiently creative, to be integrated one day into the conventional wisdom. Rubin's total contempt for the generally esteemed institutions of his culture is not a message that is easily received by those who value and cherish the very institutions that he defames. His audiences have typically failed to be receptive to his incredible theatre, and the man-in-the-street has not particularly enjoyed the demonstrations that Rubin and his cohorts have brought about. As we move into the seventies, however, Rubin's basic theme of capitalistic rip-off and government-by-cheats-and-fools is becoming progressively more meaningful. The man-in-the-street has grown intolerant, not only of Rubin but also of the objects of Rubin's theatre, the absurdity of government criminality. More and more the courts are turning to the prosecution of those who violate the public trust, rather than those who trust the public enough to violate it.

As Rubin says, he is a child of "Amerika," the off-spring of apple pie and motherhood and McDonald hamburgers. He likewise fancies himself to be in the tradition of those revolutionary nuts who created the Boston Tea Party and refused to honor and obey the unjust laws of a distant governing body. The fathers of the American Revolution were a little oddball, too, and Rubin is also a child of that intense longing to be free of oppression and to find one's own way in the world. Although he is offensive and abrasive, he invites us to examine the sources of oppression with ourselves as well as the forces of evil within the institutions that we cherish. Jerry Rubin's scathing behavioral satires of American government, his ostentatious eagerness to paint the word "F U C K" on his forehead for all to be offended by, his insistence on calling cops "pigs," his ongoing mockeries of American political processes—these are not merely the ravings of a lunatic and a "sickie." The tactics of revolutionary theatre were a form of authentic social and political protest in an age that had grown complacent and needed to be shocked into action.

It is perhaps only coincidental that on the day that I completed this chapter, Richard M. Nixon announced his resignation from the office of president of the United States. Lyndon B. Johnson's decision not to seek a second term has often been related to the intensity of the war protest during his administration. I doubt that Jerry Rubin and the movement can be credited with the resignation of two presidents, but there can be no doubt that Rubin's demonstration of the power and capacity of revolutionary theatre was an influential force in creating a mood for honesty in government. Rubin is an oddball who has helped put politics in perspective. He has been a brake on a government run awry. His ability to be himself, his own outrageous self, culminated in a necessary madness, necessary, that is, from the standpoint of social change in the sixties. Like all men, oddballs included, Jerry Rubin is a product of his times, but more oddballingly so, more individually so than most of us have been.

Part Three

Oddballs
in the Arts

8 Igor Stravinsky

"Music Hath Charms..."

IT IS GENERALLY conceded that one of the foremost means of self-expression available to a human person lies in an act of artistic creation. The arts, in both obvious and subtle ways, represent avenues of stylized individuality, and sophisticates, as well as dilettantes, take pleasure in the recognition and understanding of the unique moods and signatures of different artists. In his creations, the artist finds the prospect of communicating the most highly idiosyncratic aspects of his or her unique style of experiencing the world, and the act of creation gives both vent and form to the inchoate promptings of an inner vision and the solitary mind's eye.

Music, painting, writing, sculpture, dance, and the like are surely a form of release but they are likewise a form of statement about the human condition. The arts typically involve a subtle interplay between the artist's own unique consciousness of life and his ability to render his solitary sensitivity meaningful to others. In the purely aesthetic and creative sense, an artist is successful to the extent that he or she can bring to completion in the form of a work of art the conscious and unconscious rudiments of inner sensitivity. Insofar as a completed work faithfully represents the intention of the creator, the artist has been true to his or her sense of self and successful in that endeavor.

Artists, however, do not work in a vacuum and the reception of one's creative stirrings by the artistic public is central to the creative process. No matter what we might like to believe about the indestructible bohemian character of artists, they are very much dependent on the approbation of others for their very sustenance. The arts are as conventionalized as any other form of human endeavor, and it is not surprising to discover that every art form has highly developed rules and regulations of acceptable self-expression. In the main, *ars gratia artis* is truly an oddball ideal. Artists, too, like to be well-received and meaningfully understood and appreciated by their public, and the more individualized the artist becomes, the more likely the prospect that he will stray from the very sources of his sustenance. Most successful artists achieve fame and fortune by their ability to create a forum for their own work. If an artist can achieve a forum for his work and still maintain the integrity of his artistic spirit, he may well be on the road to genuine oddballlitry. In effect, we are saying that the authentically creative artist is of necessity a highly individualized person and that the first suggestions of this individuality typically run counter to the established norms and expectations. In the following pages, we will briefly examine convention and unconvention in the arts as personified in oddball genius.

On the 29th day of May, 1913, a truly unusual event took place at the generally stuffy and composed-to-the-point-of-boredom Paris Opera House. The usually reserved and utterly genteel patrons of music and ballet found themselves engaging, quite spontaneously and without any malice aforethought, in what can only be described as a full-scale riot. Eyewitness descriptions of the event bring back memories and visions of the prison movies of the 1930s with Jimmy Cagney, George Raft, and Humphrey Bogart banging their tin cups and wooden knives in staccato rhythm on the tables of the prison mess hall, shouting, "We ain't eatin' this slop no more, Warden!"

But the patrons of the Paris Opera House on that eventful evening in May were not prison inmates. They were not college students on a spring rampage. They were not political revolutionaries protesting an unjust government. They were, rather, just ordinary mild-mannered *Parisiennes*, known far and wide as the epitome of true cool, the very *originateurs* of the expression "*c'est la vie!*" And yet, they were being driven out of their music-loving gourds, forming factions of supporters versus antagonists, engaging in fights in the aisles in order to demonstrate their respective enthusiasm or contempt for the new musical composition and ballet being presented. The occasion was the initial performance of *Le Sacre du Printemps*, a ballet set to the novel musical perspectives of an exciting young Russian composer, Igor Stravinsky.

In the early 1900s, Igor Stravinsky (1882-1971) was a struggling, young, Russian composer who was seeking to gain a foothold in the traditions of European music. Although his father, an opera singer, had advised him to study the law, at the age of twenty-two he succumbed to the urging of master-composer Rimsky-Korsakov to take up music as his life's work; the young Stravinsky accepted the offer of the aging master to guide his training, and from this brief apprenticeship came a conventional symphony—the *Symphony in E-Flat*, Opus 1, written in 1907—and the more inspired *Scherzo Fantastique* (1909). When Sergei Diaghilev (1872-1929) heard the *Scherzo*, he asked Stravinsky to write a work for the Ballet Russe de Monte Carlo. Diaghilev, the famed Russian impresario, was in the process of organizing a group of extraordinary artists who dreamed of producing spectacles of dance, music, and decor. *Le Sacre du Printemps (The Rite of Spring)* was Stravinsky's response to the invitation of

Diaghilev. "This request changed the course of Stravinsky's career and, in consequence, that of twentieth-century music."[1] Their collaboration, along with that of world-famous dancer Vaslav Nijinsky, would eventuate in the unheard-of riot at the Opera House.

Several eyewitness accounts of that memorable evening have been preserved for musical posterity. *The Rite of Spring*, a strikingly original composition of dissonant sounds, is an evocation of pagan Russia, presenting two fundamental ideas: the primitive belief in the holiness of spring and the consecration of a maiden. The ballet itself thus drew on primitive barbaric rituals, perfectly suited to the strident impulses of Stravinsky's composition. On that momentous evening in May, the tradition-loving theatergoers sensed Stravinsky's radical departure from cherished musical values, and all hell literally broke loose. A young American music critic, Carl Von Vechten, who was present that night tells us that the curtain had barely risen when the audience began falling into factions:

> A certain part of the audience, thrilled by what it considered a blasphemous attempt to destroy music as an art, and swept away with wrath, began very soon after the rise of the curtain to offer audible suggestions as to how the performance should proceed. Others of us, who liked the music and felt that the principles of free speech were at stake, bellowed defiance. It was war over art for the rest of the evening . . . and the orchestra played on unheard, except occasionally when a slight lull occurred. The figures on the stage danced in time to music they had to imagine they heard and beautifully out of rhythm with the uproar in the auditorium. . . . I was sitting in a box in which I had rented one seat. . . . Three ladies sat in front of me and a young man occupied the place behind me. The intense excitement under which he was laboring, thanks to the potent force of the music, betrayed itself presently when he began to beat rhythmically on the top of my head

with his fists. My emotion was so great that I did not feel the blows for some time. They were perfectly synchronized with the beat of the music. When I did, I turned around. His apology was sincere. We had both been carried beyond ourselves. . . .[2]

Von Vechten and his drummer friend were not the only ones who felt carried away. Some of the audience were carried away *in ipso actu*. At the first intermission, the house lights were turned up "so that the police, who had been called in, could pick out and eject some of the worst offenders. But no sooner were the lights lowered again for the second scene than pandemonium burst out afresh, and then continued till the ballet came to an end."[3] The evening, of course, was a theatrical disaster, although the marvelous scandal created immense interest in the event as well as in *The Rite* itself.

In 1921, *Le Sacre* was played again, in concert form, at the London Concert Hall. Although the audience refrained from public riot, the music again created considerable upset in everyone present. "One alarmed listener published a letter in which he declared that the *Sacre* was a threat against the foundations of our tonal institutions." The same writer went on to aver, however, "This music will not live—and that is my only hope."[4] Wherever *Le Sacre* played in those early years, it created consternation, dismay, and public outrage. In Boston, the newspapers displayed the following jingle after its first performance there:

> Who wrote this fiendish *Rite of Spring?*
> What right had he to write the thing?
> Against our helpless ears to fling
> Its crash, clash, cling; bing, bang, bing?[5]

The very upset created by *Le Sacre*, its power to baffle and confuse, was a solid indication of its complete originality. In subsequent years, its author has come to be hailed as a genius, and *The Rite* is now understood to be the first major statement of his genius. After *Le Sacre* was staged in New York and Philadelphia in 1930, it began its increasing ascendance as a recognized masterpiece. At that time, music critic Lawrence Gilman wrote:

> This music is profoundly disquieting, —a thing of despotic power and intensity. It has the impact and something of the mystery of an elemental force. . . . This music is essentially a glorification of Spring as the supreme expression of the creative impulse—a Spring stripped bare of sentiment, austere and ruthless, yet with interludes of strange incalculable tenderness. . . . What Stravinsky has made of this conception is one of the subduing things of art . . . a thing of gigantic strength, or irresistible veraciousness. . . It teaches us again the inexhaustible responsiveness of music to new ways of apprehending life, new adventures of the imagination, new conceptions of sensibility and truth and beauty.[6]

At its initial performances, the powerful dissonance of *Le Sacre* was experienced, even by the knowledgeable music lover, as an assault upon the basic traditions of everything that music was theretofore known to be. That a musical composition could produce a riot among a group of people trained in public restraint is a phenomenal testimony to the disturbing potency of the unknown and the unique. Those first audiences were so immediately offended by its offbeat clarity, its sudden clash of rhythms and sounds, that some were jolted to attention while others revolted in action. In *Le Sacre*, Stravinsky set aside and overturned the conventions of centuries and exposed his listeners to a completely novel experience that literally set them outside of themselves. Stravinsky cannot take full credit for that momentous evening at the Paris Opera House. Diaghilev, Nijinsky, Cocteau, and others were also involved in this startlingly unique event. But Stravinsky can take credit for a lifetime of exceeding originality, and on this count the study of oddballs has much to gain from him. In Stravinsky's case, the study of oddballs is identical with the study of genius.

Igor Stravinsky has long ago moved to the ranks of the recognized masters of music, and he has achieved in his long life the very heights of professional and public acclaim. The recognition of his genius, however, was slow in coming and for many of his early years he was regarded by the musical establishment as a freak, unworthy of serious attention. Throughout his career, however, Stravinsky has seldom strayed from the path of his own individuality; though he has moved in many directions, each of his many altered paces was always peculiarly his own. Igor Stravinsky is an idiom unto himself, and it is his very individuality that has been the source of so many refreshing developments in the music of the twentieth century. In a slender volume commemorating Stravinsky's eightieth birthday, Paul Henry Lang makes the following observation:

> There are a few powerful figures in whom the main strands of music history seem to knot themselves before diverging again to form a new pattern. Igor Stravinsky, whose birthday we are celebrating, is a knot, —and a mighty hard one—of this kind. Right now Mr. Stravinsky is all the mode. His early works, after the customary time lag of some forty or fifty years, are well liked by the public, his latest, the dodecaphonic, vastly admired by the progressive professionals. But the aging master has demonstrated that it is possible for the modish to retain their individuality, for he has retained his.
>
> Such a long and distinguished career, punctuated by the most unexpected and exciting tangential departures from the norm, was bound to evoke criticisms that run the gamut from one extreme to another, yet neither those who see in the great Russian composer the deliverer of latter-day music, nor those who regard him a composer of "nihilistic motor music" are right. What Mr. Stravinsky sought above all throughout his many metamorphoses of style was an opportunity and frame for the exercising of a powerful musical instinct, ever alert, original, always seeking new outlets. He did not want to deliver but to conquer, he did not want nihilism but a

most exquisitely *raffine* game in which he created an idiom that is irreducibly his own, an idiom that for half a century has fascinated friend and foe alike, and without which the music of our century would have taken an altogether different turn.[7]

Lang notes well, I believe, a simple fact: it was Stravinsky's adherence to his own personal idiom, his sensitivity to his own heartbeat, that acted as the font of creativity, a creativity that revised old traditions in the birth pangs of the new. The history of music will be forever indebted to his originality. We are here interested, however, in the sources of his originality. What was it in Stravinsky that enabled him to be so constantly creative and highly individualized in so many of his endeavors? Why has he been so strikingly original, so marvelously oddball, in so many of his works?

Since the advent of dynamic psychology in general, and psychoanalysis in particular, it has become customary for the interested observer to interpret the singular events of one's adulthood in terms of the ongoing dynamic difficulties of one's childhood. Biographers more and more are making use of the psychohistory as a means of understanding the lives of their subjects, and various types of unconscious motivation are advanced as the underlying reasons and pushes in the achievements of adulthood. Stravinsky's biographers have been subject to the same temptations. Eric Walter White, for example, makes a psychological interpretation regarding the composition of *The Rite of Spring:*

> The powerful originality of *The Rite of Spring* represented an important personal victory gained by Stravinsky over the inhibitions of his miserable childhood. For years he had tried to revolt from the stultifying restrictions of his family life; and now that he had succeeded in doing so in terms of artistic expression, it was particularly appropriate that the image that precipitated his release should have been that of spring— "the violent Russian spring that seemed to begin in an

hour and was like the whole world cracking," and which, by his own admission, was the most wonderful event of every year of his childhood.[8]

White, perhaps rightly so, underlines the artistic originality of *Le Sacre* as a symbolic break with Stravinsky's personal inhibitions. The difficulty with such interpretations, however apt and appropriate they might be, is that they fail to crystallize the very sources of individuality. Was it a dire childhood that *enabled* Stravinsky to be so incredibly, albeit violently, original in the composition of *The Rite*? Was it the rigid mores of a bleak peasant home that accounted for the artist's lifetime of constant metamorphosis into new forms of musical creativity?

No one set of explanations is sufficient to the awesome reality of Stravinsky's creativity, of course, but there is something about Stravinsky that renders him remarkably similar to the other oddballs in this study. And that is his consuming eagerness to seek and define the convention and then to flaunt it, to do the opposite of what the convention requires and demands. In this, Stravinsky is also magnificently oddball.

There can be no doubt that Stravinsky is a committed strayer from convention, that he uses the convention as the point of departure for the expression of his individuality. *The Rite of Spring*, for example, moves almost totally away from the established principles of harmony and gives vent instead to Stravinsky's experimentation with dissonance, with sounds that clash instead of harmonize. The crude fearlessness and primitive quality of *The Rite*, which is scored in the throbbing passions of dissonance, is not merely a sample of the unpolished rebelliousness of youth. Late in his life, in a filmed interview, Stravinsky would declare, "I adore dissonance."[9] Stravinsky's music is so wonderfully original because of his constant attempt to defeat the listener's expectations, to provide novelty, and to deal with the unknown and the unexpected.

Edward T. Cone has written at length on Stravinsky's personalization and distortion of musical traditions and patterns. It is worth quoting him in context:

> The persistent vitality of conventional patterns in music has often been noted. Whatever the reasons for their original development, one advantage of their use is clear: in an art both abstract and temporal they furnish signposts to aid the listener, who can neither turn back nor pause to look around him. The danger, of course, is that the composer will use them as a crutch; and it is true that the academic conception of the forms as molds has encouraged the production of much facile and un-distinguished music. But when, as during the period of the Viennese Classics, original musical thought and generally accepted procedures find not only mutual accommodation but mutual reinforcement, the results are happy for composer and audience alike.
>
> The acceptance of conventions presents another possibility, which is my concern here. A composer may deliberately defeat the expectations aroused by the specific pattern followed; the resulting tension between the anticipated and the actual course of the music can be a source of esthetic delight. This is the way Stravinsky has used conventions. . . .[10]

This is much the way Jerry Rubin presented himself to the House UnAmerican Activities Committee. Knowing that the House expected anyone giving testimony to appear in suit and tie, Rubin caught them all off guard by appearing in the uniform of an American Revolutionary soldier, the resulting tension itself testifying to the absurdity of everyone involved. Stravinsky uses conventions as a means of demonstrating their power to rob us of unknown pleasures by welding us to our respective sticking places. When we expect the next note to go up, Stravinsky will deliberately take us down, and we are left to deal with our own foolishness.

Throughout his distinguished career, Stravinsky has

shown an enduring capacity to unearth and develop the novel and the unusual. His inquiring mind never takes anything for granted, and he is constantly involved in the exploration of oddball perspectives. His originality as a composer is clearly due to his manifest inability to leave well enough alone. The great Russian composer is a tinkerer, a meddler, a toyer, a player, a man who constantly delves into his own patterns to examine and re-examine the inner workings of his own musical soul. If Stravinsky had been a professional golfer, his first act would be to carve up a golf ball and unwind its rubber-band innards. As a professional composer, he cannot accept anything even so basic as the musical scale! As Eric Walter White has observed, "Throughout his composing career, he has never taken anything for granted. For him the most obvious things in music, such as the intervals of the scale, have needed a re-examination and testing that has stripped them of their jejune academic attributes and given them fresh life."[11]

Stravinsky's tendency to question and analyze the commonly accepted aspects of any situation has given him an almost absolute freedom from fashion as well as a firm dignity in the face of pressures of influence. In 1938, for example, the musical score from *The Rite of Spring* had been "borrowed" by Walt Disney as the musical accompaniment for the prehistoric section of Disney's new cartoon film *Fantasia*. As Stravinsky became known to Hollywood, all sorts of offers were made to engage him in many of Hollywood's less-than-artistic productions. In his *Memories and Commentaries*, he describes a situation in which he was offered $100,000 "to pad a film with music." When he refused, he was offered the same fee to allow someone else to write some music in his name![12] He again refused, demonstrating the manner in which he had become free of even economic influence. And yet, his independence of artistic spirit shows even more integrity than his offbeat economics.

Musically, Stravinsky's freedom from fashion has expressed itself as a constant sensitivity to his own gyroscope. "I want to suggest neither situations nor emotions, but simply to manifest, to express them. . . . Though I often find it extremely hard to do so, I always aim at straightforward expression in its simplest form. I have no use for 'working out' in dramatic or lyric music. The one essential thing is to feel and convey one's feelings."[13] Stravinsky's comments on the expression of the artist and the nonexpression of the music itself has aroused considerable controversy among the critics. On another occasion, he exclaimed:

> For I consider that music is, by its very nature, essentially powerless to *express* anything at all, whether a feeling, an attitude of mind, a psychological mood, a phenomenon of nature, etc. *Expression* has never been an inherent property of music. That is by no means the purpose of its existence. If, as is nearly always the case, music appears to express something, this is only an illusion and not a reality. It is simply an additional attribute which, by tacit and inveterate agreement, we have lent it, thrust upon it, as a label, a convention—in short, we have come to confuse with its essential being.[14]

Stravinsky's understanding of music is more than a mere negation of the Wagnerian and Hitlerian conception of music as an expression of a national mentality. The Russian composer is saying more than this. He is saying that there is nothing conventional about music itself but rather that the conventions and the expectations are brought to it by the listener. The underlying structure and tempo of an artistic piece are no more than the artist's attempt to convey his own purely individual feelings and understandings. Just as it is the task of the artist to purify himself of the accretions of his own habits, so it is the task of the listener to purify himself of his inner expectations. In short, neither creator nor receiver can be fully alive if each is not open to the prospect of discovery, of finding something new, rather than merely demonstrating to each other the tried and the true. In his music, then, Stravinsky constantly treats his listeners to the unexpected, which is a means of growth for all.

In his *Poetics of Music*, Stravinsky maintains that the source of all creativity is the inclination of the artist to exercise "the principle of speculative volition,"[15] which is merely the artist's appetite to discover something new and different. For himself, he admits that this appetite to explore the unknown and discover something new is a periodic natural need that regularly brings him to new bursts of creativity and continuing discovery. In his *Expositions and Developments,* Stravinsky shares with Robert Craft an ever-recurring event in his dream life. He reveals a regularly recurring dream in which he is forever trying to tell the time and forever looking at his wristwatch, only to discover that it isn't there.[16] His biographer, Eric Walter White, suggests the possibility of an anxiety neurosis connected with his creative potency.[17] I guess the very marvel of a genuine oddball constantly tempts one to psychiatric diagnosis, but for my own part Stravinsky's dream is no more than a symbol of his lifelong search to discover his own idiomatic self. And when you're well-involved in self-discovery, you can never be sure, even of the time of day.

From the point of view of the study of oddballs, the genius of the Russian composer brings to light some hints at the underlying dynamics of authentic, creative individuality. In Stravinsky's music we find an utter distrust in convention, manifested as a rejection and disbelief in absolute values. In his artistic compositions, this disbelief in absolutes has enabled him to seek out himself and find his own meanings, free from the dictates of fashion and convention. There are, of course, manifest differences between life and art, but I wonder whether we have merely been trained to believe in such differences. Is not life itself, individually and creatively lived, merely a more dramatic demonstration of artistic creation? Does not every man write and rewrite, on an almost daily basis, the composition of his own person? And can we not write and rewrite the scripts of our ongoing existence in any fashion that we choose? Must we live and have our being only according to the socially defined methods of our group? Are we not free to be as we wish to be? In the oddball, at least, one senses the thrill of discovery in life as well as art.

Stravinsky teaches yet another lesson. Oddballs need not be angry and foul-mouthed flaunters of convention. One need not be antagonistic toward one's social group in order to develop a unique and creative style of one's own. Stravinsky is a gentle man. When he violates a convention or an expectation, his intent is clear: to enlighten, not to offend. He is a man who knows the traditions of art, and of life, quite well, and he has a happy familiarity with the common expectations. He is able to stray so creatively from the straight and narrow only because he knows it so well. He has a deep and abiding respect for tradition, but he does not worship tradition as a means of avoiding his own responsibility to develop himself as well as the traditions of his art. Stravinsky has aligned himself with various traditions only as a means of creating something new of them and for himself. This highly individualized artist demonstrates with exceeding clarity the means by which convention can serve as the springboard to one's own individuality and self-fulfillment as well as the creation of something new and different. And I am still left to ponder whether art is so different from life.

9 James Joyce
The Devil's Advocate

My recollections of my brother go back to such early years that I hardly dare say how far back they go—at any rate to nursery days. I have a recollection, definite enough though vague in detail, of a dramatic performance of the story of Adam and Eve, organized for the benefit of his parents and nursemaid. I was Adam and a sister, my elder by less than a year, was Eve. My brother was the devil.

Stanislaus Joyce
My Brother's Keeper

James Joyce was to play the devil for most of his life, and if not the devil, then at least the devil's advocate. Perhaps the leading novelist of the twentieth century, his writings have stirred as much controversy as could possibly be expected from the written word. Joyce is a complex, disquieting figure, and the harsh symbolism of his errant consciousness continues to hang like a giant shadow over contemporary letters. To fathom his mind and style is to enter a labyrinth from which there may well be no return. Many have said that

Joyce is more a blind alley than a labyrinth, and this most complex of authors is unquestionably the most difficult and enigmatic writer in the history of fictionalized narrative. And Joyce planned it that way.

There is no convenient starting point in the consideration of an artist as elusive and illusive as James Joyce. The volumes of critical literature on his life and writings long ago reached the stage of being appalling and yet they continue to grow. Each new volume or article, moreover, seeks to find some new slant, some different interpretation of Joyce's style and meaning. Whether laudatory or deprecatory, every English literature professor in the world seems to have penned his own personal theory of one or another of Joyce's books. Although he has been dead for over three decades, Joyce's presence in contemporary letters is still keenly felt and very much alive.

James Joyce was born on February 2, 1882, in Dublin, Ireland, and died on January 13, 1941, in Berne, Switzerland. Although he was certainly a son of Hibernia, Joyce hated the provincialism of his native land and fled Ireland at his earliest opportunity; he lived all of his adult life in self-imposed exile from the land of his origins, the "tribal Irish playpen" that will live forever in his writings. His most productive years were spent in the literary haunts of foreign lands—in Paris, Zurich, Trieste—but all of his writings were concerned with the sounds and sights and feels and smells of his native Dublin. Joyce's life was not unusually eventful, although he lived in Europe during the two world wars that shook the continent to its very foundations. He was not particularly productive in his craft, although he shared the companionship of most of the great writers of his time. Joyce never allowed secondary events—like critical reviews, the opinions of his literary friends, or world wars—to interfere with the accomplishment of the oddball plan that he conceived in his youth and executed throughout his adulthood. For these reasons, his literary legacy is less voluminous than that of many less-accomplished and less-renowned authors. He published a few, small collections of poems, the best known of which are *Chamber Music* (1907) and *Pomes Penyeach* (1927). Early in his career, Joyce brought a volume of *Chamber Music* to the famed Irish poet A.E. Housman for critical comment. "Young man," A.E. is reported to have said, "there is not enough chaos in your mind."[1] This was a fault that Joyce would certainly correct in his later writings, which are the source of his claim to fame in the archives of oddballitry.

The *Dubliners* (1914) is a series of short stories or character sketches of Dublin natives; although the book was completed in 1906, Joyce would not allow any of the prospective publishers to change a word of his composition, which eventuated in the book's passing through twenty-two distinct rejections. In a letter to Bennett Cerf, Joyce pointed out:

> You are surely well aware of the difficulties I found in publishing anything I wrote from the very first volume of prose I attempted to publish: *Dubliners*. Publishers and printers alike seemed to agree among themselves, no matter how divergent their points of view were in other matters, not to publish anything of mine as I wrote it. No less than twenty-two publishers and printers read the manuscript of *Dubliners* and when at last it was printed some very kind person bought out the entire edition and had it burnt in Dublin—a new and private *auto-da-fe*.[2]

Joyce's reception at the hands of various publishers may well be the reason for the relative paucity of his literary output. At any rate, he seems to have maintained his sense of humor despite his difficulties with publishers and editors.

His difficulties with *Dubliners* were actually minor compared to the problems he would encounter with later manuscripts. *A Portrait of the Artist as a Young Man* (1916) is a marvelously readable book but was first published only with the kind help of a friend. *Ulysses* (1922) secured Joyce's distinction as the most oddball novelist in history and has proved to be the most controversial book ever written. *Finnegans Wake* (1939) was fifteen years in the writing and yet is most assuredly the most obscure book in all of letters. Joyce's dedication to this mysterious work consumed almost the whole of his creative energy during the time that he was becoming recognized as an outstanding writer. *Portrait, Ulysses,* and *Wake* remain his major writings, and his progression as an increasingly innovative novelist in these three works is possibly the most studied phenomenon among contemporary literary scholars. For our own purposes, either *Ulysses* or *Finnegans Wake* is sufficiently strange in itself to include Joyce in a study of oddballs, but the combined impact of these two works thrusts Joyce to the head of the list.

From his earliest days, it was clear that Joyce would struggle mightily to distinguish himself as different from his fellows. Mary Colum, who would become his close friend and author of a very revealing biography, recalls her initial meeting with Joyce:

> Some time afterward I had my first glimpse of James Joyce: he was pointed out to me in Kildare Street, where the National Library was. My companion remarked, "There is James Joyce, the great genius of University College in his own estimation." He had already taken his B.A. degree, I was told, and in modern languages as if he were a girl student, for the girls at this time were supposed to be specialists in modern languages and literature, while the boys' domain was classics, mathematics, and similar masculine pursuits. Neither this information nor the appearance of James Joyce was engaging, and the odd rumors we heard about him at the time were very shocking to our young naivete. He had given up religion, it was said, and went in for evil frequentations of all kinds.[3]

Even in his youth Joyce had already developed a good deal of that special oddball quality that rendered him suspect and unusual to other members of his social group. In turn-of-the-century Dublin, James Joyce was questioning the roots of his Catholic religion and had, in fact, "lost the faith," a rather singular event in a city of unquestioned (and unquestioning)

Catholicism. It wasn't as though Joyce had gone over to the other side. In Dublin, there was no other side, except for that which was represented in the minds of parishioning Catholics as Satan and hell-fire. Thus, Joyce was seen by other university students as being in league with the devil.

In later years, someone would ask Joyce whether he had turned to "some other religion," to which he replied, "I have lost my faith, but I have not lost my mind."[4] His intense early training by the Jesuits had instilled in him both the best and the worst of Catholicism. Joyce could never give up the intellectual elegance of the Catholic faith, and his training on Thomas Aquinas continued to manifest itself in even the most desultory and tangential ramblings of his later writings. The apparent chaos of *Ulysses* and *Finnegans Wake* belies an underlying orderliness not unlike the smooth clarity of Catholic doctrine. And yet, Joyce seems to have been in life-long rebellion against the faith of his ancestors, and Catholic imagery continued to haunt his consciousness to his dying days. Despite his public break from the Church, Joyce could never quite excise the Catholicism from his own unconscious; as far as the Church was concerned, Joyce seems to be much more the devil's advocate* than the devil himself. But more importantly, Joyce is a devil's advocate for all of mankind.

In those same student days, Joyce presented his perception of Ireland as an amazingly provincial land. In 1901, he published privately a paper entitled "The Day of the Rabblement," which he had intended for the college magazine only to find it rejected by the Jesuit adviser. This essay

---

*In the Catholic Church, a "devil's advocate" is someone appointed by the Church to act as a guardian of the Church's integrity. For example, when a member of the Church is being considered for sainthood, the function of the devil's advocate is to pursue disbelief and literally "dig up as much dirt" as possible on the person in question. In this way, the Church insures that it will honor only those who can survive even the devil's advocate, thus showing that they are truly worthy of being dignified and honored by the Church.

was a fairly scurrilous, albeit accurate, attack on the provincialism of the Irish theatre which was dedicated exclusively to the production of patriotic plays by nationalistic authors. Joyce's university days thus began in him a process of revolt against both Catholicism and provincial patriotism, which he considered to be the *bete-noire* of Ireland. In 1904, he met Nora Barnacle and soon fell in love with her. Since he was opposed to marriage as an institution and could not live with Nora in Dublin, he decided then and there to leave Ireland for continental Europe. Nora would be his lifelong companion, finally entering into a civil marriage in 1931.

A Portrait of the Artist as a Young Man is a fictionalized autobiography of Joyce's young adulthood and vividly portrays his own attempts to overcome the paralyzing conventionality of family, religion, and homeland. The central character of *Portrait* is Stephen Dedalus, and Joyce here appeals to the mythical figure of Daedalus, the builder of the Cretan labyrinth in Greek legend as well as the inventor of wings that enabled him and his son Icarus to escape imprisonment in the very labyrinth that he had built. The figure of Daedalus haunts all of Joyce's works, just as Joyce's own life is an attempt to achieve freedom by flight from the labyrinthine grip of social control. *Portrait* is a marvelously successful autobiographical novel and Joyce succeeds in attaining an utterly detached view of himself. *Portrait* is thus a pruning and hybridizing of actual fact and artistic license in the attempt to discover and communicate a base of meaningful truth. As David Daiches has pointed out,

> In Joyce the traditional bohemian rejection of middle-class respectability combined with his sense of the inadequacy of the environment in which he grew up to reinforce the critical position he first developed in his student days, that the true literary artist, "like the God of creation, remains within or behind or beyond or above his handiwork, invisible, refined out of existence, indifferent, paring his finger nails." Only by remaining thus

aloof can he achieve that comedy of multiple identification, that simultaneous taking of all points of view,
which is Joyce's way of solving the problem of selection
and significance.[5]

In *Portrait*, then, Joyce achieves the wonder of an
almost objective view of himself, seeing himself as imbedded
in the customs of family, religion, and homeland, and yet ever
sensitive to the inborn tensions between his needs for self-
discovery and the expectations of his social group. Through
the figure of Stephen Dedalus, Joyce sets forth his plan of
stepping beyond determinism, of excising the sources of
influence both from without as well as from within. *Portrait* is
more than a characterization of a young man's trials and tribulations, it is a blueprint of a path to freedom, which in
Joyce would lead him to produce the most unconventional
literature ever written.

Dedalus' systematic rejection of family, friends, country, and religion begins to move with startling rapidity as the
prospect of self-imposed exile takes shape. Near the end of
Portrait, Stephen tells his companion Cranly:

> Look here, Cranly . . . You have asked me what I
> would do and what I would not do. I will tell you what I
> will do and what I will not do. I will not serve that in
> which I no longer believe, whether it call itself my home,
> my fatherland, or my church: and I will try to express
> myself in some mode of life or art as freely as I can, using
> for my defence the only arms I allow myself to use—
> silence, exile, and cunning.[6]

At another point, young Stephen exclaims, "You talk to me
of nationality, language, religion. I shall try to fly by those
nets." Stephen Dedalus expresses Joyce's need to express
himself in both art and life in complete, unfettered freedom.
His exile from Ireland gave him the physical means to escape
the pressures of family, church, and country, and in his
writings the maturing Joyce would find the means "to fly by

the net of language" as well. *Portrait* sums up both the nature of Joyce's revolt as well as the nature of his resolution.

In *Ulysses*, the nature of his life's plan and artistic intent begins to manifest itself more clearly. *Ulysses* is an alarmingly original book, both in style and content. The work displays Joyce's increasing indifference to public canons as well as his increasing involvement in the innards and the unknowns of human consciousness; it is an intensely introspective examination of "human insides," of the mysterious vagaries and problems of the human mind and its inner experiences. Stephen Dedalus is again present but only secondarily so, as a witness to the novel's protagonist Leopold Bloom, a boorish and lower-class Dublin Jew; it is a day that will live forever in literature as "Bloomsday," June 16, 1904. Bloom's introduction in the novel comes quite unexpectedly and without fanfare: "Leopold Bloom ate with relish the inner organs of beasts and fowls," and this after a clear allusion to the fabled Ulysses. Joyce's intent is unmistakable: to portray the cherished virtues of the supreme warrior in the homeliness of the "nitty-gritty" Bloom. Bloom is no Babbitt. Bloom is truly Ulysses, and Joyce would have us believe that so is every man, no matter what the meanness of our hidden, private lives. Joyce believed that, like himself, every man is unique and every man is a Ulysses in constant search of a home that he can call his own. In Bloom, Joyce would turn the humdrum and the ordinary into the exciting and the extraordinary.

> Bloom is unusual in his tastes in food, in his sexual conduct, in most of his interests. A critic has complained that Bloom has no normal tastes, but Joyce would undoubtedly reply that no one has. The range of Bloom's peculiarities is not greater than that of other men.
>
> At the same time, Bloom maintains his rare individuality. His responses to experience are like other people's, but they are wider and cleverer. Like Ulysses, though without his acknowledged fame, he is a worthy man. Joyce does not exalt him, but he makes him

special. Aldous Huxley says that Joyce used to insist upon a "thirteenth-century" etymology for the Greek form of Ulysses' name, Odysseus; he said it was a combination of *Outis*—nobody, and *Zeus*—god. The etymology is merely fanciful, but it is a controlled fancy which helps to reinforce Joyce's picture of the modern Ulysses. For Bloom is a nobody—an advertisement canvasser who, apart from his family, has virtually no effect upon the life around him—yet there is god in him.[7]

Joyce would expose all of humanity through Bloom, both in its godliness as well as its deviltry. The hidden private life, the deep dark side of human nature, would emerge in Joyce's hands as no writer before or since could make happen. Joyce would act as the devil's advocate for man himself, still seeing man as worthy no matter how awful the thought or deed, finding in Bloom a sense of godliness and magnificence superior to any hint of evil or degradation. In the service of the majesty of every man, Joyce would bring out and set forth every form of lowly thing that all the mechanisms of social restriction struggle to repress. Thus, Bloom masturbates and defecates and urinates before our very eyes. And Joyce would argue that in spite of every lowly thing, Bloom was yet majestic. Thus, *Ulysses* begins with a pointed blasphemy of the Catholic mass and ends with a wandering sexual reverie of Bloom's wife, recording in vivid detail her lust for every hand that has ever been placed on her in a lust equal to her own. In its seven hundred and more pages, Joyce treats the reader to a kaleidoscope of no-no's, carefully developed in the most original of styles.

Ulysses is the first major literary achievement of the stream-of-consciousness style, in which Joyce develops the device known as the interior monologue. The work moves back and forth from narrative to, quite unexpectedly, the disjointed and unverbalized perceptions of the characters. It is difficult reading because it is an attempt to portray the inelegant recesses of conscious and unconscious mind. By means of this highly unusual style, Joyce achieves some singular distinctions. For example, *Ulysses* contains the longest sentence ever written in the English language, which by my count runs to twenty-four full pages in the 1961 Modern Library edition. This is even more unusual when one considers the fact that this sentence is preceded by the second longest sentence ever penned, running to a mere twenty-one pages. It is possible, of course, that the period following the first sentence might have been just a flyspeck on the original manuscript, in which case the sentence would have run to over forty-five complete pages. Needless to say, Joyce's style tends to suspend most of the conventional rules of grammar!

In *Ulysses*, Joyce attempts a formidable, if not impossible, undertaking: he tries to give an objective, literary presentation of subjective, human experience. As David Daiches has observed, Joyce invites the reader to participate in the great conundrum of human existence. Daiches reads Joyce's invitation as follows:

> Look at Leopold Bloom as he argues with a drunken Dubliner in a pub; look again and you will see that he is not Leopold Bloom but a heroic figure of mythology wrestling with a giant; look yet again and you will see that he is not heroic at all but ludicrous and fantastic; and look yet once more and you will see that the actual, the heroic, and the ludicrous do not represent separate values, have no permanent meaning, but are simply angles of vision on a single, yet all-embracing fact: I am showing you all life, to which all adjectives, and therefore no adjectives, are applicable, something which is, that neither appeals nor disgusts, that neither elates nor depresses, that I have no relation to beyond merely observing and that you have no relation to beyond reading the product of my observation.[8]

In order to help the reader experience and share in his developing metaphysics of experience, Joyce of necessity produced a highly unusual book. The publication of *Ulysses* was, of course, a major scandal, and we will not here recount its many trials and tribulations. Suffice it to say, *Ulysses* was banned as obscene in every country that tried to bring it to the public. For many years, it was available only as an underground volume and then to a relatively exclusive group of *literati*. The rapid shifts from narrative to stream-of-consciousness rendition, the proclivity to engage in gutter language, the depiction of explicit sexual tendencies—in short, all the devices by which Joyce brought the character of Bloom to life—all these proved much too unconventional to allow the book easy access to the public.

And yet, *Ulysses* would have its eventual victory even in the courts. In the United States, New York District Court Judge John M. Woolsey pronounced on December 6, 1933, that *Ulysses* was not obscene and that there was no legal reason why *Ulysses* should not be published and distributed to the reading public. Judge Woolsey's decree, which was rendered in the same week as Congress's repeal of Prohibition, was hailed as a landmark in free expression and "the new deal in the law of letters." The decree is brilliantly developed and shows considerable insight into Joyce's intents and purposes. Quoting freely:

> In writing *Ulysses*, Joyce sought to make a serious experiment in a new, if not wholly novel, literary genre. He takes persons of the lower middle class living in Dublin in 1904 and seeks not only to describe what they did on a certain day early in June of that year as they went about the City bent on their usual occupations, but also to tell what many of them thought about all the while.
>
> Joyce has attempted—it seems to me with astonishing success—to show how the screen of consciousness with its ever-shifting kaleidoscopic impressions carries, as it were on a plastic palimpsest, not only what is in the focus of each man's observation of the actual things about him, but also in a penumbral zone residual of past impressions, some recent and some drawn up by association from the domain of the subconscious. He

shows how each of these impressions affects the life and behavior of the character which he is describing . . . .

It is because Joyce has been loyal to his technique and has not funked its necessary implications, but has honestly attempted to tell faithfully what his characters think about, that he has been the subject of so many attacks and that his purpose has been so often misunderstood and misrepresented. For his attempt sincerely and honestly to realize his objective has required him incidentally to use certain words which are generally considered dirty words and has led at times to what many think is a too poignant preoccupation with sex in the thoughts of his characters.

The words which are criticized as dirty are old Saxon words known to almost all men and, I venture, to many women, and are such words as would be naturally and habitually used, I believe, by the types of folk whose life, physical and mental, Joyce is seeking to describe. In respect of the recurrent emergence of the theme of sex in the minds of his characters, it must always be remembered that his locale was Celtic and his season Spring.

Whether or not one enjoys such a technique as Joyce uses is a matter of taste on which disagreement or agreement is futile, but to subject that technique to the standards of some other technique seems to me to be little short of absurd.

Accordingly, I hold that *Ulysses* is a sincere and honest book and I think that the criticisms of it are entirely disposed of by its rationale.[9]

Joyce, as devil's advocate, had been vindicated, and the dirty word would be preserved in print for all posterity.

Near the very end of *Portrait*, Stephen Dedalus tells his friend Cranly:

". . . I do not fear to be alone or to be spurned for another or to leave whatever I have to leave. And I am not afraid to make a mistake, even a great mistake, and perhaps as long as eternity too."

Cranly, now grave again, slowed his pace and said:
"Alone, quite alone. You have no fear of that. And
you know what that word means? Not only to be
separate from all others but to have not even one
friend."

"I will take the risk," said Stephen.

In *Ulysses*, Joyce proved to be courageous and offbeat
enough to run the risk of censure and misunderstanding,
which came freely to him. Judge Woolsey's decision was a
hallmark in the process of his vindication, and *Ulysses* is now
regarded as one of the greatest novels ever written. If Joyce
had not attempted to fly over the nets of all conventions—if
he had not been oddball—he would have been pleased to
languish in the orderly world of Irish Catholicism, with a mind
lacking in chaos.

But Joyce would prove to be yet an odder-ball. He had
not really flown by the "net of language," and he was still
driven to break loose from even the most necessary conventions of sensible, communicative language. In *Finnegans
Wake*, Joyce flies over the net of language. The book was
written over Joyce's last seventeen years, during which he
suffered a crippling eye disease as well as intermittent
poverty. That he brought this work to completion is a
miracle. That it is read and understood, however, is even
more a miracle. *Finnegans Wake* is a concatenation of
riddles, wrapped up in enigma, shrouded in confusion,
leading to a massive conundrum. Adaline Glasheen has
remarked that the book ". . . is a model of our universe
which is mysterious as a whole and in its parts. Joyce is
therefore mysterious in his turn . . . . It was conceived as
obscurity; it was executed as obscurity; it is about obscurity."[10] It certainly seems very obscure to me, and it is a
pleasure to find one's opinion supported by the experts.
Although *Ulysses* is esoteric in many of its moods and
passages, *Finnegans Wake* is frankly unintelligible. This
immensely abstruse work may well be the format of a highly

unique vision, but it makes such incredible demands on the reader that few are able to read through to the end, let alone understand to any significant degree that which they have read. Its advocates, however, proclaim a great love for this book, while other accomplished scholars regard it as a completely oddball work.

The very least accomplishment of Joyce in *Finnegans Wake* is the creation of an entirely new language, Finneganese or Joycese or oddballese or what-have-you. Though an initial reading might give the impression of double talk—not unlike an old Abbott and Costello routine—the language of *Finnegans Wake* is carefully constructed. An Irish wake, of course, is a spectacle to behold and one finds quite an unusual language spoken there; the wake is an event in which grief for the dead and joy for the living are equally mingled in mourning and festivity. To describe a wake, Joyce, for example, coins the word "Guinesis," combining "Genesis" and "Guiness," the Bible and drink, which is stout enough for any creation.[11] The language of *Finnegans Wake*, unlike that of *Ulysses*, is not so much execribbly profansive as it is immensibibly difficuloo, with a bit of Tippicanoe and Tyler too, boo-hoo, boo-hoo.

A typical passage in *Finnegans Wake*, in this instance a deliberate mix-up of historical events, reads as follows:

> . . . This is Rooshious balls. This is a ttrinch. This is mistletropes. This is Canon Futter with his popynose. After his hundred days' indulgence. This is the blessed. Tarra's widdars! This is jinnies in the bonny bawn blooches. This is lipoleums in the rowdy howses. This is the Willingdone, by the splinters of Cork, order fire. Tonnerre! (Bullsear! Play!) This is camelry, this is floodens, this is the solphereeens in action, this is their mobbily, this is pannickburns. Almeidagad! Arthiz too loose! This is Willingdone cry. Brum! Brum! Cumbrum! This is jinnies cry. Underwetter! Goat strip Finnlambs!

This is hard to read! As Daiches says, "This is the human

scene as described by one who has abandoned all standards of significance."[12] Napoleon, Wellington, and Almighty God are faintly recognizable amid the horseplay, puns, and confusions, but one must wonder what Joyce was possibly hoping to accomplish in this reduction of all the known conventions of distinction and difference to some orgy of poppycock talk, i.e., toppypalk or whatever. There are no more than a few easily intelligible sentences in the whole of the book, but the book is certainly not just a matter of Gaelerish (i.e., Gaelic gibberish) or Celbishior (i.e., Celtic rubbish, either). The hybridizing of languages, the running together of ideas, the juxtaposing of historical events—these are all devices by which Joyce seeks to depict the underlying unity and interconnectedness of all mankind in the totality of subjective experience. Joyce's attempt to fly above the distinguishing conventions of language in the creation of a unique language is a way of saying that there are no real distinctions between men and yet every man is unique.

The structure of *Wake* is that of an elaborate dream, with all the vicissitudes and disassociations of dream mechanics and dream symbolism. It is, in effect, an elaborate and extended symbolic commentary on all mankind, indeed, the very underpinnings and substrata of human experience. In *Wake*, Joyce attempts to get at what Coleridge called "the realms of inmost being" or what Jung referred to as "the collective unconscious." Joyce can no longer tolerate the procrustean manipulation of reality into conventional symbols or even ordinary language. Thus, *Wake* moves at the level of a dream, a massive symbolic dream of mankind's history and its very innards. Homer Obed Brown has, I think, captured much of the essential meaning of this mysterious work:

> Because mind is a matrix of all possible incarnations of the human spirit in all possible and past myths and stories, and in all possible selves, the book is a dream containing all of history and every identity is endless

metamorphosis. Here Joyce created a language into which all languages are condensed, a primordial dream language always at the point of dissolution, which at once mimics the multiplicity of experience, "represents" it, and yet creates it anew. The dream of pure archetypal form incarnating by a necessary synecdoche all possible meanings: "I, entelechy, form of forms . . . . "[13]

Wake is Joyce's means of demonstrating his insights into the nature of his own oddballing as a fundamental and universal character of man. He is saying that in its sources the human spirit is much too wide and extensive to be confined and pent up by any set of social conventions; that all we have to do is fall asleep and we will find our own individual spirit in active rebellion against the conventional events of our day; that our dreams can tell us who we really are; that there is something about us that defies characterizations of right and wrong, of good and evil, of god and devil. *Wake* is Joyce's attempt to understand and portray the human condition beyond and without the jaundice of a prejudicial view, having flown over the nets of family and friends, of religion, of nationalism, indeed of language itself.

Finnegans *Wake* has probably attracted far more detractors than supporters, but those who like it gambol about it like huge sheep dogs filled with enthusiasm for their master. A. Walton Litz avers:

Finnegans *Wake* is a supremely serious work, not an elaborate literary joke or a fashionable experiment. It is also a supremely rational work . . . . His purpose was to construct a mythology in which any detail of human behavior—past, present, or future—could be related to the cycles of history. Thus Joyce was pleased when after the publication of Finnegans *Wake*, the Russian invasion of Finland seemed to parallel one of its leading motifs. [Litz is here referring to the recurring motif of father-son conflict, but, in Joyce's words, remember the "Finnlambs?"] The work's ability to process new material had been confirmed.

> *Finnegans Wake* is certainly the most difficult book
> in the English language, and it is likely to remain so for
> some time . . . . But *Finnegans Wake* is a unique
> achievement; it is unlikely that the combination of
> talents and limitations which produced the *Wake* will
> ever occur again.[14]

On the other hand, those who do not like Joyce and his work often achieve considerable heights of hostility in registering their complaints. As we have seen in this study of oddballs, the unique and the highly individualized are often met with outrage and upset by the protectors of tradition and convention. A very balanced criticism from the negative position is represented, however, in a letter to Joyce from the famed English historian and scientist H.G. Wells. This letter is so telling that it is worth quoting in its entirety:

> Lou Pidou, Saint Mathieu,
> Grasse, A.M.
> Nov. 23, 1928

My dear Joyce,

I've been studying you and thinking over you a lot. The outcome is that I don't think I can do anything for the propaganda of your work. I've an enormous respect for your genius dating from your earliest books and I feel now a great personal liking for you but you and I are set upon absolutely different courses. Your training has been Catholic, Irish, insurrectionary; mine, such as it was, was scientific, constructive and, I suppose, English. The frame of my mind is a world wherein a big unifying and concentrating process is possible (increase of power and range by economy and concentration of effort), a *progress* not inevitable but interesting and possible. That game attracts and holds me. For it, I want language and statement as simple and clear as possible. You began Catholic, that is to say you began with a system of values in stark opposition to reality. Your mental existence is obsessed by a monstrous system of contradictions. You may believe in chastity, purity and the personal God and that is why you are always breaking out into cries of cunt, shit and hell. As I don't believe in these things except as quite personal values my mind has never been shocked to outcries by the existence of waterclosets and menstrual bandages—and undeserved misfortunes. And while you were brought up under the delusion of political suppression I was brought up under the delusion of political responsibility. It seems a fine thing for you to defy and break up. To me not in the least.

Now with regard to this literary experiment of yours. It's a considerable thing because you are a very considerable man and you have in your crowded composition a mighty genius for expression which has escaped discipline. But I don't think it gets anywhere. You have turned your back on common men, on their elementary needs and their restricted time and intelligence and you have elaborated. What is the result? Vast riddles. Your last two works have been more amusing and exciting to write than they will ever be to read. Take me as a typical common reader. Do I get much pleasure from this work? No. Do I feel I am getting something new and illuminating as I do when I read Anrep's dreadful translation of Pavlov's badly written book on Conditioned Reflexes? No. So I ask: Who the hell is this Joyce who demands so many waking hours of the few thousands I have still to live for a proper appreciation of his quirks and fancies and flashes of rendering?

All this from my point of view. Perhaps you are right and I am all wrong. Your work is an extraordinary experiment and I would go out of my way to save it from destructive or restrictive interruption. It has its believers and its following. Let them rejoice in it. To me it is a dead end.

My warmest good wishes to you Joyce. I can't follow your banner any more than you can follow mine. But the world is wide and there is room for both of us to be wrong.

Yours,

H.G. Wells[15]

The approach of H.G. Wells to both life and letters is, of course, considerably more prosaic than that of Joyce. And he is quite correct; the world is quite large enough for conventionalists like Wells, also oddballs like Joyce. And yet, Wells fails to grasp much of what Joyce is about. He thinks that Joyce's genius was merely a result of circumstance, an accident of fate; that Joyce was unfortunate enough to have had thrust upon him a set of values that were in stark opposition to reality; that Joyce's literary contributions and philosophy were merely an attempt to break out of the monstrous value system that had been foisted on him in his youth, like some kind of awful canard; that Joyce's oddball experiments in consciousness and language and "reality" were merely a function of his rigid, Jesuitical upbringing in Irish Catholicism, which he could never quite escape. Wells, for all his openness to Joyce, has much of the smugness of the ardent traditionalist, the latent belief that his own traditions and conventions are more correct, more in touch with the "real" reality.

Despite the Wellsian judgment, however, Joyce had come to grips with the forces of social determinism in his life—the genuinely powerful traditions of family, country, and church—in a way that Wells could not, for Wells speaks as though Joyce were a victim of circumstances but he, Wells, were not. At the very least, Wells seems to maintain that the conditioning forces and determinisms in his life were so favorable or benign as to be noncontrolling and nondetermining—conventions that don't conventionalize! In the paradox of James Joyce, Wells' view of himself—which to me is an amazing statement of self-righteousness—is merely another angle of vision; and yet, Wells is as much a victim of convention as the self-conscious Stephen Dedalus, whether Wells sees it and acknowledges or not. But Wells is Bloom as well. And Bloom is Ulysses.

One of the major themes of Joyce is the equivalence of all reality, the underlying interconnectedness of all realities, no matter how disparate they might seem. In order to develop this more inclusive vantage, it was necessary for Joyce to shed the jaundiced vision—perhaps, "monstrous value system"—of a more restricted view. Joyce is certainly not the first Irish Catholic to leave Irish Catholicism behind him in a quest for liberation. But what Joyce has come to in the stead of Irish Catholicism is the real marvel. Joyce is the devil's advocate for Irish Catholicism as well as himself. And for Wells as well. In the Joycean vision, there is, in the end, nothing monstrous about Irish Catholicism, despite his need to fly beyond its apparently constraining nets. For Irish Catholicism itself is merely another angle of vision, neither good, nor bad, nor indifferent.

Wells would understandably have difficulty seeing this paradox in Joyce. As Herbert Howarth has observed about Joyce, "A characteristic of his art is to use popular conventions and codes, ideals, language, and toys, in a form accessible only to those who have otherwise turned away from them."[16] One must question one's roots and sources in order to gain some meaningful "angle of vision" on oneself, as well as on others. If one has not questioned one's own sources—family, country, religion, or whatever—it is difficult to realize the full majesty of one's resources, the conventional values and attitudes of the social group that sustain one's daily life. Flying beyond the restrictions of convention does not necessarily entail the ultimate rejection of convention.

Each man leaves the reading of James Joyce with his own interpretations and judgments. This is as it should be. No right or wrong. No more correct or less correct. Scholars may quibble over the fine points. Some, like H.G. Wells, may reject his work as utter foolishness. And rightly so. Or wrongly so. It makes no difference. Such is the paradox of James Joyce. Absolute values are replaced by relative values and absolutely so. Bloom is Ulysses.

To me, Joyce is neither more nor less than beautifully oddball. He does not force me to question whether there *are* any genuine and meaningful standards of significance. Rather, he nudges me to consider which standards are significant to me. He does not ask me to abandon convention and tradition but rather to see convention and tradition for what they really are, "angles of vision" for the endless array of expression that is humanity. Else, like Ulysses, life itself is a seemingly endless voyage of unknown nets and hidden snares.

10 Lenny Bruce

A Shaman
in a Sham World

IT WAS SPRING 1962 in London, England. The Establishment, London's only cabaret theatre, had been going strong for several years. Founded as a private club to avoid the censorship of the Lord Chamberlain's office, the Establishment had quickly become a roaring success. The manager, Peter Cook, had sensed infallibly the appetite of the urbane, young Londoner for daring, improvisational satire. Cook was himself a member of *Beyond the Fringe,* a group of four, wonderfully zany, young comedians who excelled in caustic satire of British propriety. *Beyond the Fringe* made regular ventures onto the Establishment's stage, as did a host of talented new performers who delighted their audiences with a broad range of humorous invective and well-directed sarcasm. This was no-holds-barred entertainment, and the patrons of the Establishment were seldom upset by anything that transpired upon its slender stage.

The Establishment, however, was now in an uproar. Each evening there was an inevitable series of walkouts and fist fights. The patrons were offended by what they were hearing and seeing, and they were registering their displeasure, indeed their outrage, by taking to the aisles in physical acts of protest. It was like Stravinsky's *Rite of Spring* all over again. Some of the walkouts were more notable than others. Yevegeny Yevtushenko, the Russian poet, left in a huff. So did John Osborne, the "angry young man" playwright, and Penelope Gilliatt. These were not stuffy conservatives; these were "liberated" people, artists who had made their own tracks in the world. Siobhan McKenna, the noted actress of stage and screen, led her party of eight from the club, and at the door she had her escort punch Peter Cook right in the nose. Why was everyone getting their respective noses out of joint, in both the figurative and literal sense?

On the stage each night, a strange event occurred. A slim and slightly built young man, dressed in a Nehru suit, would venture into the spotlight and begin talking to the audience. Nothing more. Just talking. Sometimes he would be so inaudible, he seemed to be talking only to himself; when he could be heard, however, the audience would break, often simultaneously, into screams of protest and howls of laughter. He was just a performer, a standup comic, who had a strange power with words, a power that could produce in his listeners both instant laughter and instant outrage. As his "performance" continued, it became increasingly apparent that he was a free-wheeling, verbal acrobat of an entertainer, ranging glibly and with malice aforethought on every offbeat topic under the sun. He was encouraging people to smoke marijuana because it did not induce lung cancer. He was speaking out in favor of pornography for children because it was healthier than learning about sex from Hollywood or prudish parents. He was pointing out that publicity was stronger than sanity: given the right public relations pitch, armpit hair on female singers would become a national fetish. He was underlining the duplicity of all political systems: if Norman Thomas, the esteemed socialist, was ever elected president, he would have to find some minority to hate in order to stay in power—in which case, his campaign slogan might well be "Smack a midget for Norm." He was undermining the church, politics, family, the whole bailiwick of accepted values, and he was doing so with pointed and consummate skill. Many in the audience were offended. It was Lenny Bruce at his awesome best, and he was provoking his listeners to fits of righteous indignation.

Lenny Bruce, in his brief stint in England, was sufficiently shocking to the British Establishment and establishment that he was soon declared an undesirable alien and escorted from the country. He had gone beyond the fringe. All because of words softly spoken under a nightclub spotlight. The noted British critic, Kenneth Tynan, was himself roused to a fit of dithers at the action of the British authorities; Tynan had some words of his own:

> Constant abrasive irritation produces the pearl: it is a disease of the oyster. Similarly—according to Gustave Flaubert—the artist is a disease of society. By the same token, Lenny Bruce is a disease of America. The very existence of comedy like his is evidence of unease in the body politic. Class chafes against class, ignorance against intelligence, puritanism against pleasure, majority against minority, easy hypocrisy against hard sincerity, white against black, jingoism against internationalism, price against value, sale against service, suspicion against trust, death against life—and out of all these collisions and contradictions there emerges the troubled voice of Lenny Bruce, a nightclub Cassandra bringing news of impending chaos, a tightrope walker between morality and nihilism, a pearl miscast before swine.[1]

Such eloquence in defense of an "undesirable alien"! What a marvelous capacity Lenny Bruce must have had to turn people on and turn people off. Whatever might be said for or against him, there can be no mistaking his gift for ringing the chimes of his fellow man.

Lenny Bruce was an oddball of considerable proportions. Since his untimely death in 1966 at the age of forty, the myths surrounding this many-sided man have been swollen beyond all proportion to reality. Lenny was an entertainer, a caustic funny man and standup comedian who did his act in the shoddiest burlesque houses as well as the most elegant nightclubs. For a brief period in the late fifties and early sixties, his light shone bright in the circles of public entertainment and he was hailed as a comic genius. He was also unceremoniously thrown out of foreign countries, arrested by the police in the very midst of a performance, prosecuted in the jurisdictional courts of three different cities for the flagrant nature of his public language, and convicted of obscenity for words that he spoke on the public stage. In his later years he literally spent more time in the courtrooms of the American judicial system than he did in the performance of his art. (Perhaps, it would be more correct to say that the courtroom became his public theatre of performance.) Following his tragic death, he has been increasingly eulogized and cultified as a social hero, a magnificent contemporary shaman who sought to purify and cleanse American culture of the demons of false conventions and counterfeit ideals. Although many sought to ban him from the stage, others saw him as the moral conscience of America and its foremost teller of truth. Long before Howard Cosell discovered the theatrics of Monday Night Football, Lenny Bruce was credited with "telling it like it is."

Who was Lenny Bruce? To be sure, he was a remarkably complex man who inspired complex reactions in others. Like most oddballs, however, Lenny came from humble and unspectacular origins. He was the only child of the broken marriage of Mickey Schneider and Sally Marr (nee Sadie Kitchenberg). In his early years, he was passed back and forth between his father, a plodding jack-of-all-trades businessman, and his mother, a lifelong lesser light in show biz. At the age of nine, the young Leonard Alfred Schneider settled down to a reasonably normal upbringing in a little frame house in Freeport, New York, a home only recently purchased by his father and newly acquired stepmother. It is said that his father was terribly overindulgent and spoiled him rotten. At any rate, Lenny left home at the age of seventeen to join the Navy and defend his country in the midst of World War II. After two years of life aboard ship, his patriotism began to wane, and he became desperate to leave the Navy at any cost. Eventually he hit upon a scheme that would set him free. Albert Goldman, in his remarkably balanced biography of this remarkably unbalanced man, notes as follows:

> One day soon, Lenny was going to go into the crew's shower when it was filled with other men and start to grab the guys' cocks. He was always impersonating fags; there were even men who thought he was a fag—very well, he would use that prejudice to get himself a discharge. When the men complained to their officer, he would confess that he was a queer, that he longed to have sexual relations with men, and he would stick with this story until they gave him a discharge. It would probably be a dishonorable discharge—he didn't give a damn.[2]

Lenny's decision to dismiss the social considerations that might be involved in being labeled a homosexual in favor of his immediate need to leave the Navy prompted him to act out his little plan. He was discharged from the Navy in the fall of 1945, imprinted with the prospect of doing the outrageous deed in order to get his own way.

Throughout the late forties and early fifties, Lenny was at work sprucing up his act. Show business would be his chosen profession and he would practice the art of the standup comedian. He began as a mimic doing a series of fairly inaccurate impersonations of stock Hollywood characters, but his mimicry would always find some very minor aspect of his target and blow it all out of proportion. Lenny could not make it as a mimic because he was too spontaneous, too undisciplined to hang in with some rigid format. Soon he was leaning toward more spontaneous comedy.

His early years in the business found him developing his presence as a stage funnyman in various dimly lit, out-of-the-way if not off-the-map nightspots or acting as a master of ceremonies on the bump-and-grind circuit. His peers and colleagues were the street people, a motley assortment of seedy characters, small-time hoodlums, strippers, prostitutes, pushers, and an occasional luminary on his way to the big time. Certainly not the breeding grounds to produce a new and more refined version of the *Ave Maria*! These were people, however, who were adept in knowing what was allowed and what was off limits. The police were constantly in the background, and it was necessary to know what you could get away with and what you couldn't get away with. Lenny never learned. He had to try to get away with everything.

More and more, Bruce became convinced that the whole of life was a gigantic hustle, and ever-expanding rip-off. In his autobiography, *How to Talk Dirty and Influence People*, written as he was beginning to emerge as a celebrity, Lenny proclaims his inchoate insight into the essential dishonesty of the human condition:

> If the Messiah were indeed to return and wipe out all diseases, physical and mental, and do away with all man's inhumanity to man, then, I, Lenny Bruce—a comedian who has thrived both economically and egotistically upon the corruption and cruelty he condemns with humor, who spouted impassioned pleas to spare the life of Caryl Chessman and Adolf Eichmann alike, who professed the desire to propagate assimilation and thereby involve integration—would in truth know that I had been a parasite whose whole structure of success

depended on despair: like J. Edgar Hoover and Jonas Salk; like the trustees, wardens, death-house mainten-ance men, millions of policemen, uniform makers, court-recorders, criminal-court judges, probation officers and district attorneys whose children joyously unwrap Christmas presents under the tree bought with money earned by keeping other men from seeing *their* child's face beam at a cotton angel, who would have been without jobs if no one in the world had ever violated the law; like the Owl-Rexall-Thrifty Drugstores, crutch-makers, neurological surgeons and Parke-Lilly employees on the roof of the Squibb pharmaceutical house, ready to jump because the blind can see, the deaf can hear, the lame can walk; like the ban-the-bomb people who find out there really is no bomb to ban and they don't know what to do with their pamphlets. The dust would gather on all the people who hold that superior moral position of serving humanity, for they will have become aware that their very existence, creative ability and symbolic status had depended wholly upon intellectual dishonesty. For there is no anonymous giver, except perhaps the guy who knocks up your daughter.

In the movies, Porter Hall and Gene Lockhart were always successful businessmen, but Everett Sloane was a *tycoon*. He would get his gun off disillusioning Joel McCrea, who wanted to publish a newspaper that would make a statement, and telling him: "M'boy, you'll see when you get old that it's all a game." And I used to think "No, it's not that way, this cynical old bastard is bull-shitting, there *are* the Good Guys and the Bad Guys, the liars and the truth-tellers."

But Everett Sloane was right.

There is only what *is*. The what-*should*-be never did exist, but people keep trying to live *up* to it. There is only what *is*.[3]

There is in Bruce's cynical, street-wise ethics much food for thought and self-examination. This is Lenny at his best, telling it like it is, pulling down the top-heavy super-structures of phony morals and self-righteousness. This is Lenny Bruce, involved with man, struggling with the human dilemma, trying to make sense of the shabbiness and inherent sinfulness he is convinced must lurk beneath the hide of everyman. This is Lenny the exposer, the moral conscience of mankind, insisting that we get in touch with all the evil inherent in the way the world works. This is Lenny accusing, pointing a finger at our self-deceits, and his as well. In these days of his transition from Nobody to Somebody, Lenny is a marvelous screwball, ready to show us up for what we are.

He was an outrageous stunt-maker, incurably addicted to the put-on. One of his favorite tricks in those days was to bring a live telephone on stage with him and get into some spontaneous piece with a poor, benighted recipient of his call. Goldman relates the dialogue from one conversation when he placed a call to the maitre d' at Ciro's, one of the most elegant dinner spots in Los Angeles:

> "Hello? Is this Ciro's? Yea? Well, we're from out of town. It's our last night in Los Angeles. The Andersons from Cedar Rapids told us to be sure and stop in and see your show. But me and the wife have only $1.75. Would that be enough, do you think?"
>
> . . . .
>
> "Well, suppose I stand up at the bar and let Minnie, that's my wife, sit down and order some coffee?"
>
> . . . .
>
> "Well, wait a minute! Would it be all right if I came in the doorway and let Minnie sit in the car? Then I could tell her later all about the show."[4]

This was Lenny laying it all bare—the refreshing naivete of the small towner, the elaborate vanity and pseudosophistication of the posh nightclub, the questioning playfulness of an inquisitive social commentator.

After years of playing master of ceremonies on the burlesque circuit and its dreary routines, Lenny began competing with the strippers themselves. One of his competitions became an overnight, show-biz legend. After waiting in the wings and watching one particularly buxom stripper tease the audience for what seemed to be an eternity, and then scampering off still partially clothed in the most interesting places, Lenny did the honest thing and treated the audience to the real McCoy. Before walking back onstage to introduce the next act, Lenny prepared for a serious social statement:

> Out came that talented, handsome, witty, and vivacious M.C., Mr. Lenny Bruce—*bare-assed naked*! Walking slowly across the stage toward the mike, a painfully bored expression on his face, Lenny called out—barely stifling a yawn—"Let's give the little girl a big hand!" Then he demonstrated exactly what he meant by plopping his hands together exactly twice.[5]

Now that we have arrived in the enlightened era of the mid-seventies where streaking is an accepted fact of life, few eyebrows are raised at the spectacle of public male nudity. Imagine, however, what it must have meant for a struggling young comedian in the late 1950s to parade his male chauvinistic honesty in the very arena of womanly dissimulation. Whenever Lenny felt that things were getting a little too stuffy, he could always be counted on to strip to the buff and dispense with all signs of affectation.

He had, however, an even more remarkable knack at getting other people to peel in public. Goldman relates a typical incident:

> One night Lenny found himself being heckled by a drunken woman who was later identified as the mother of a famous movie star. With the encouragement of the audience, he coaxed the woman up onstage and began his counterattack by insisting that her voluptuous figure was padded. She answered proudly that her body was better than any of the strippers on the bill. "Then go on, dear," Lenny urged, "take off your dress and show us!" Without waiting to be asked twice, she started taking off

her clothes and didn't stop until she was naked except for her underpants. She wasn't jiving, as it turned out—her figure was dynamite! Lenny began singing the opening notes of "Night Train." As the woman began to sway her hips and go into a strip routine, Lenny seized her clumsily and began doing a really horny dance. Between steps, he tore off his jacket, tie, shirt, and was going for his pants, when the two stumbled and fell, rolling across the stage. The audience gave them both a big hand.[6]

To Lenny it was all the same. Whether saying some words or doing some deeds, whether stripping himself bare or stripping someone else bare, whether teasing an individual or mocking an institution, Lenny could see no differences, no distinctions, which separated one form of human behavior from any other form of human behavior. Bruce was a consummate amoralist driven to explode the myths of social class and demanding that his audience act out with him his need to demonstrate his perception of a world filled with ostentation and devoid of genuine values. It was this sense of everything's-the-same-and-nothing-is-sacred that would give Bruce the ability to set aside any inhibition in his programmatic exploration of human equivalence. What others might do in the privacy of their homes, however, Lenny would do with increasing recklessness on the public stage. It was another way of saying, "Why be dishonest? This is how I am in private so why should I be any different when I appear onstage?" Lenny was well on his way toward becoming a self-appointed public exorcist of private taboos.

Bruce's genuine penchant for unfailing honesty in this regard slowly earned him the reputation of a modern Diogenes. At his best, he was an incredibly glib hipster executing polished satires of sham values and sacred institutions. His biographer, Albert Goldman, rightly characterizes the essence of Bruce's comedic art as "a single comprehensive metaphor for human experience" in which the religious, political, and social leaders of the world—the very pinnacles of human accomplishment and achievement—are viewed as equivalent to the earthy, hustling characters of Bruce's immediate show biz experience. This simple equation enabled Bruce to expose the whole of human culture—the veritable "it all" of reality—to the single touchstone of the hustle. In his most celebrated routine, *Religions, Inc.*, he imagines that the "religious" leaders of the world—Billy Graham, Oral Roberts, Patamunzo Yogananda, Rabbi Wise, General Sarnoff—had gathered together for a sales conference in San Francisco.

Bruce begins the routine with all these majestic characters reminiscing about the days before they "got religion" and were all exceedingly poor, and he has them counting all the profits from their current enterprises: cocktail napkins printed with "Another Martini for Mother Cabrini," a genuine Jewish-star-lucky-cross cigarette lighter combined with a glow-in-the-dark mezuza, and so on. Pretty soon, Oral Roberts takes a collect call from the newly elected Pope John and answers the phone, "Hello, Johnny! What's shakin', baby!" On and on Bruce goes exploring the hypothesis that organized religion is big business and that behind the closed doors religious leaders are no different from hustling advertising men engaged in an astoundingly successful rip-off. (The publication of the Nixon tapes, by the way, has tended to lend added dynamite to Bruce's irreverence for political bigwigs.) Behind his cynical impiety and barbed wit, however, Bruce at his best was able to capture a certain believability that left the listener both laughing and pondering, as well as angry and upset. Bruce's satire was more like a shotgun than a high-powered rifle, going after everything within range, and his comedy routines had a way of getting beneath the skin of everyman, exposing hidden prides as well as unanalyzed but fiercely held beliefs. Lenny forced people not only to think about themselves but also to question the simple realities that are too often the function of an unquestioning faith. Like all the great satirists from Juvenal to Jonathan Swift, Lenny was all too eager to rub the nose of his fellow man in values and realities that were blindly held sacred. As the show-biz magazine *Variety* pointed out early in Lenny's career, his penchant to satirize everything in an unrestrained fashion would eventually lead him to offend someone better left unoffended. In England, he was just thrown out of the country, but in America he began to get arrested. Regularly. During the month of October 1962, Bruce was arrested three different times in Los Angeles for using obscene language in a public place. His battle with the courts had begun; constitutional government had declared war on him.

In November 1962, Bruce made his own official declaration of war. He moved to Chicago to appear at the Gate of Horn, and he ominously entitled his show *Let the Buyer Beware*. Lenny Bruce was no longer an entertainer. He had become a crusader, locked in mortal combat with the powers-that-be over right and wrong, freedom and coercion, good and evil, the individual and the group, health and sickness, sanity and insanity, truth and untruth. Bruce had become a man with a mission, exposing the clay feet of every idolatrous belief, unearthing the underlying shakiness of all human institutions, ripping at the hypocrisy and self-righteous moralism that pits man against man, nation against nation. Lenny Bruce was learning what it meant to be a victim, and it was clear that his sympathies were with the underdog. Any underdog would do, for Bruce was beginning to see that man's inhumanity to man was ever-recurring.

Newspaper headlines at the time were rife with reports of Gary Powers, the U-2 pilot who had been shot down over Russia and had subsequently confessed to the Russians the exact nature of United States espionage. The patriots were indignant at Powers for his traitorous behavior. Bruce went after the self-delusion of the supposed patriot with excoriating precision; in the midst of his act, he would suddenly raise the question of whether Powers was a traitor and spring into an imaginary dialogue between patriotic citizens:

"Goddamit, I'd never sell my country out!"

"You ever been tested?"

" . . . I'm just not the kind of guy that would. I know it. I'd never sell my country out. Powers is a fink. That's why I'm gonna cast the first stone: he's no good. A wrong guy, bad apple. If I get on the jury, I'll burn his ass. And he's going away for a long time. That's it, no bull-shit. I've got secrets right here. I'm a loyal American. No, I'd never sell my country out."

"They got the other guy? They got his pants down? But I don't give a goddam what they do to him, I'd never sell—What're they putting a funnel in his ass for? Can't put a funnel in his ass! Geneva Conference! Tell 'em to take the funnel out—they can't do that . . . What're they heating up that lead for?"

"You're not getting these secrets from me! Forget that with those tricks!

"They wouldn't put hot lead into that funnel that's in that guy's ass, now, would they? For a few dumb secrets! Would they? Would they? . . . they are? . . . well, that's ridiculous!"

"Oh, the secrets? Surprise! Here they are buddy! I, ah, I mean I got more secrets, too, you wouldn't even believe! These are bullshit secrets. I'll make up shit. I'll give you the President and the White House!

"I just don't want to get hot lead in my ass, that's all. . . ."[7]

This was not standard nightclub entertainment. Bruce was raising chilling questions about man's honesty with himself. At times, he would become deeply philosophical. He began reading an adaptation of a poem by Thomas Merton, the Trappist monk:

My name is Adolf Eichmann.
The Jews came every day
to vat they thought vould be
fun in the showers.
The mothers vere quite ingenious.
They vould take the children
and hide them in

bundles of clothing.
Vee found the children,
scrubbed them,
put them in the chambers,
and sealed them in.
I vatched through the portholes
as they would dahven and chant
    "Hey mein Liebe, heyyyy."
Ve took off their clean Jewish love-rings,
removed their teeth and hair —
for strategic defense.
I made soap out of them,
I made soap out of all of them;
and they hung me,
in full view of the prison yard.
People say,
    "Adolf Eichmann should have been hung!"
Nein.
Nein, if you recognize the whoredom
in all of you,
that you would have done the same,
if you dared know yourselves.
My defense?
I vas a soldier.
People laugh
    "Ha ha! This is no defense,
    that you are a soldier."
This is trite.
I vas a soldier,
a good soldier.
I saw the end of a conscientious day's effort.
I saw all the work that I did.
I, Adolf Eichmann,
vatched through the portholes.
I saw every Jew burned
und turned into soap.
Do you people think yourselves better
because you burned your enemies
at long distances

with missiles?
Without ever seeing what you'd done to them?
Hiroshima . . . Auf Wiedersehen![8]

At the conclusion of the recitation, Bruce would scream out in a deep cry of anguish and disappear from the stage, leaving the audience confused and reeling from the emotional impact of the poem. His "Let the Buyer Beware" was as much an invitation as a challenge: "If you recognize the whoredom in all of you, that you would have done the same, if you dared know yourselves." Lenny Bruce had become a prophet and a shaman, invoking the spirits of the nether world of mankind's unknown inner self: "If you dared know yourselves . . . ."

At the Gate of Horn, Bruce was arrested again for using obscene language in a public place. It was said that his blasphemous comments on Catholicism had offended the predominantly Catholic bureaucracy in Chicago government. As Goldman points out:

> Eventually, the trial took on the form of a Catholic inquisition: with a Catholic judge, a Catholic prosecutor, and an all-Catholic jury, every one of whom showed up on Ash Wednesday with a black smudge in the middle of his forehead. [The judge had to order the jurors to remove the mark in court.] As Brendan Behan remarked at the time: "That scares *me*—and I'm Catholic!"[9]

In a highly controversial trial, Bruce was convicted in Chicago, and the remainder of his life was literally spent in the courtroom attempting to defend his art from the long arm of the law. His career was ended. A few short years later, he was dead, perhaps by his own hand.

It is said that beneath the surface of every great comedian is an equally great tragedian, that comedy and tragedy are only other sides of the same coin. Bruce was a tragic comedian, in his life as well as his art. There is no need to rhapsodize this point, but in Lenny Bruce the tragic and the comic are frighteningly close to being one and the same.

His public howls of laughter were indistinguishable from his private howls of pain; in the moods that he would create in a rapt audience, there was but a short step from the tickle to the tear, from hilarity to rage, and from rage to outrage.

There was much pain in the life of Lenny Bruce. The coroner's report indicates that he died an accidental death at the age of forty due to an overdose of drugs, probably heroin. Dick Schaap's afterword to *How to Talk Dirty* attempts to take the sting out of this grim reality, telling us "he wasn't a junkie. He wasn't strung out. He just wanted, on August 3, 1966, a taste of stuff. It was his last supper."[10] Bruce may or may not have been a Messiah, but he was certainly a junkie. Goldman's biography makes it abundantly clear that Bruce's need for drugs was frantic and compelling and consumed much of his adult life. Lenny's comedy and social commentary were blended in the crucible of intense personal experience; the turmoil of his inner and outer lives was incredibly intense, and he regularly sought relief from the pain and confusion of this intensity in the predictable relief of hard drugs and soft drugs and whatever kind of drugs he could get his hands on. The fact of his addiction, however, need not obscure the amazing lesson of his life. It would be fatuous to believe that Bruce could be discounted on the count that "he was just a junkie," and it would be equally foolish to dismiss the tragedy of his addiction as a critical facet in the intensity of his personal search to make sense of the complexities of existence.

Ostensibly, Lenny Bruce became a public menace because he used offensive words in public—words like *asshole, fuck, cocksucker*, etc. His use of such language in public was judged to be obscene by a jury of his peers, but Lenny Bruce had no peers. He was an oddball. He was an iconoclast. Bruce was convicted not of obscenity but of upsetting people's notion of reality. Lenny Bruce maintained that "what is" is reality and that "what should be" is a false reality, shameful and dishonest. Bruce argued that "if we dared to know ourselves" then we would find within our sense of self the traitorous Gary Powers, the mass-murdering Eichmann, and the obscene Lenny Bruce. In a single performance, Bruce could alter drastically the meaning of right and wrong, robbing people of their sense of what is right and making them feel very wrong about themselves. He was a "reality thief" who provoked people to indignation and outrage, not just with foul words but by turning over the applecart of accepted values and consensually validated reality. Perhaps he was a shaman, a modern-day exorcist, setting loose societal restraints on private thoughts, inner fears, and inmost taboos.

Lenny Bruce would do anything to shock people. Early in his career, a club audience was ignoring his performance when he suddenly stopped and shouted out: "A kid looks up at his father and says, 'Daddy, what's a degenerate?' His father looks down and says, 'Shut up, kid, and keep sucking.' And so are all of you degenerates." Shocking. Offensive. On another occasion, Bruce was appearing on a small elevated stage and was not being well-received by the audience. At which point, he instructed the houseman to turn down all the lights so that it became pitch black in the club. Bruce then threatened that he was going to urinate all over the audience, causing a minor riot. Sick. Hostile.

I have difficulty liking Lenny Bruce. He bothers me. He is upsetting to my sense of self. His total disregard for social nicety triggers things inside my gut that I would rather not deal with or rather not admit about myself. I would prefer to see him as an object lesson in failure, an oddball gone awry, individuality run haywire. I want to think that in some way he was defective in genuine humanity, that he lacked the basic ingredients of what it means to be human and civilized, that he couldn't distinguish values from garbage. But I can't be sure. Maybe Bruce was a shaman. Maybe my values are sham. What would I have done in the place of Eichmann or Powers? If someone was actually on the verge of pouring the hot lead into the funnel, what would I believe about reality at that point? Would I believe in "what-is" or rather in "what-should-be"? Or would I believe anything that the man with the funnel would like me to believe?

Lenny has been dead for over a decade, and he remains a terribly bothersome person. He was a ticking bomb of unpredictability and indiscretion. His own search for individuality took him to the nether limits of human experience, to degradation and victimization. He broke himself into pieces. Perhaps he was a sacrificial lamb. He ran the risk of being oddball and outrageously individualized—the risk of censure, persecution, ostracism, incrimination. It killed him. He exposed himself, body as well as soul, in deeds as well as words, in his raw, subjective self, and he was swallowed up by the society that he satirized. He loosed spirits and passions that he could not control, and they turned on him. He took pleasure in rubbing mankind's nose in the human condition, and the human condition did him in. At some point in his search to be free of social determinism and to be completely himself, saying and doing anything he damned well pleased, he lost respect even for himself. There is a signal lesson in the life of Lenny Bruce. The shared conventions of any given society may well be no more than the shared conventions. What some particular group of people holds to be true may well be no more than what some particular group of people holds to be true. Perhaps there is no enduring truth. Perhaps the values and beliefs of any group in time may well become vicious and demeaning even to the members of the group. Whatever. When a man discards conventions and social values, however, he chooses to march to his own drumbeat. And he had best be convinced of himself. Lenny Bruce died because he stopped believing in himself. Again, maybe he died because he stopped believing that he could be understood.

Julian Barry's play Lenny opens with a quote from the preface of George Bernard Shaw's St. Joan: "Even Socrates, for all his age and experience, did not defend himself at his trial like a man who understood the long accumulated fury that had burst on him, and was clamoring for his death; for [his accuser] had really nothing to say except that he and his like could not endure being shown up as idiots every time Socrates opened his mouth." I think Lenny Bruce understood. I think he understood that he could not be understood. He died from being too much an individual. Socrates imbibed a fatal dose of hemlock; Bruce injected a fatal dose of heroin. Both executions were neat and clean. Both were convicted of excessive abrasion of the societies in which they lived. Lenny Bruce died of an overdose of individuality.

Part Four

Oddballs
in the
Human Sciences

11 The Fabulous Fowlers and the Science of Bumps

THIS INVESTIGATION HAS adopted the point of view that commonly held conventions, traditions, beliefs, laws, and so forth are essentially guidelines that organize the experience of reality for a particular social group. Such commonalities are, of course, quite necessary to the life and continuance of any given society, although individual members of a social group may well enter into flagrant disagreement with one or another or all of the bylaws. From the standpoint of oddballitry and the science of individuality, it is important to realize that such conventions, when left unchecked and unexamined, can easily become sacred cows that hinder the development of the social group as well as the individual. The purpose of conventional values is to focus and channel the human experience, and conventional mores are ways of enhancing a clear sense of reality in what might otherwise be a very confusing world. Since such conventions do act as guideposts and milestones in "the booming, buzzing confusion," social groups must continue to develop conventions that are suited to the changing realities of social experience. In this respect, the oddball performs a useful social role because it is typically the oddball who signals the need for change.

As social realities change, conventional behavior can appear foolish and conventional values can seem ridiculous. For example, it was once considered good form for a gentleman to open the door so that a lady might be the first to enter a room. With the advent of women's liberation, however, that one-time gentleman might well have his fingers broken by that selfsame, one-time lady. It is sometimes interesting to note the apparent confusion that sets in when a liberated man and a liberated woman approach a door together!

Nor is this merely a matter of manners and etiquette. Any articulate feminist will argue well that the simple change in behavioral expectations symbolizes a complete revision in an entire set of relationships that exists between men and women. A sincere feminist will experience this change in etiquette as a redefinition of her metaphysical understanding of reality and a significant alteration in her sense of personhood. A traditional gentleman may continue to value and uphold an old-fashioned etiquette—that is, his own metaphysical understanding of reality—with a considerable degree of conviction and emotion, but he will soon be out of step with the changing realities of social experience. If he holds on to his old etiquette and metaphysics for a long enough time, he may well become an oddball! Typically, however, it is the oddball who provides the impetus for change, although some oddballs are created by the rapid changes in the social group to which they refuse to adapt. The oddball is simply someone who continues to hold out for his or her own individualistic view of reality, no matter what the conventions of the social group.

Truly individualized persons—real, genuine oddballs—are probably fewer and farther between than we might imagine. The woman who opens her own doors, for example, is no longer considered an oddball. The mores and expectations have already changed to the extent that large groups of women are developing new conventions with respect to the role of women in the world. If a woman becomes too intent on acting out a program of women's lib, she may never come to anything that is truly individual and truly her own. As conventional etiquettes and understandings dissolve, both men and women are faced with a more confusing sense of reality and are also faced with the prospect of developing a more satisfying sense of their own personhood and a more individualized sense of being. If in the midst of the confusion that is generated by changing conventions one merely reaches out and hangs on to a new set of conventions, then the new set of conventions can act as constraints and straightjackets as well as guideposts and milestones. In times of social confusion and unrest, the person who knows who he is and what he believes is more likely to become a leader-oddball than a screwball-oddball. Oddballs can also act as facilitators of social development as well as disrupters of the social order; both roles, however, are equally meaningful. The oddball is someone whose sense of reality is sufficiently different from the common experience of the social group and he is capable of modifying or expanding the experience of reality that is commonly shared by the social group.

This has been especially true in the history of the sciences. Sometimes we allow ourselves to believe that science has some special prerogative to truth that is distinct from and superior to other forms of human endeavor. The nonscientist tends to think that the scientist is able to be "more right" about his convictions than is the case with the man-in-the-street; scientists, of course, do everything they can to foster this illusion, but there is nothing about science that renders it superior to the workings of the human phenomenon. Science is a human creation which is as subject to the movements of oddballs and idols as is any other form of human endeavor. Scientists are trained to sound more erudite and authoritative than the man-in-the-street, and occasionally some scientist or another achieves some startling technological feat that lends credence and authority to the whole business of science. And yet, the scientist who is not an oddball is as conventionbound and socially determined as anyone, and the rules of scientific rigor might well act as blinders that prevent the prospect of getting beyond conventional theories and points of view. Progress in science has very much been a function of the oddball who followed his own unique vision in the establishment of something new.

In the philosophical sense, most scientists are quite willing and able to admit that the accepted theories and practices of one generation are typically abandoned by the next generation. In the nitty-gritty, however, they fight like hell to hang on to their own beliefs and conventions. One of the more flagrant examples of oddballs and idolatry was the case of Louis Pasteur. In 1880, Pasteur began publishing his laboratory observations that when an animal is inoculated with a weak culture of a germ the animal will develop an immunity to the disease even when exposed to a stronger culture. When this notion of inoculation was introduced into French scientific circles, Pasteur was made a laughingstock. How could an animal possibly be protected from a disease by actually being injected with that very disease? It seemed foolish, indeed. Pasteur's laboratory observations continued to reinforce his belief in this unique notion.

A grand experiment was thus arranged in order to test the believability of Pasteur's suggestion. The anthrax epidemic among the sheep of France had reached frightening proportions, while the French veterinarians could do little but look on helplessly. It was agreed that fifty sheep would be randomly chosen and that Pasteur would inoculate twenty-five of them with a weak culture of the anthrax virus. This public experiment was greeted by the medical and veterinary establishment with all manner of subterfuge and derision. They apparently wanted the experiment to fail! No matter that Pasteur's claims held tremendous promise for improving the human condition, his colleagues preferred that he be discredited rather than that they be forced to change their theories and practices. Despite the resistance of the scientific-medical establishment, Pasteur's experiment was astonishingly successful—the twenty-five animals that had been inoculated with anthrax remained healthy, whereas twenty-two of the twenty-five animals which had not been inoculated soon died. Pasteur's oddball theory of inoculation was vindicated, to the great dismay of the conventional science of his day. Today, inoculation and vaccination have become a way of life in medicine, and those who question their effectiveness are regarded as charlatans. (In this regard, it is interesting to note that, in the United States of the 1970s, more people die from smallpox vaccinations than actually die from smallpox itself!) The principles and discoveries of Pasteur have been incorporated into the scientific lore and are part and parcel of the standard practice of the conventional physician. Again, the offbeat and the oddballs have become the hallowed standard of a succeeding generation.

There is no need to be too hard on the scientists, however. As a movement within human culture, science typically takes great pains to maintain an objective stance toward new theories and discoveries, if not toward the conventional wisdom. When all is said and done, every science is at best a very human undertaking which is subject to the same dilemmas and vicissitudes that plague mankind in all of its magnificent subjectivity. When a scientist, no matter what his particular persuasion, violates the shared reality of his social group, when he says or does something that lies outside the conventional experience of his peers, he is regarded with the same alarm, distrust, and upset that Diogenes encountered when he went naked through the streets of Athens. Scientists are creatures of convention and the rule of truth in science is very much the power of conventional beliefs. There are no ironclad rules or laws that govern any area of human experience and investigation, and science itself is no more than a social contract among educated peers to look at things in a certain way. No matter what the layman or the scientist might believe of science as the foothold of genuine truth, science is no more than a set of human conventions in which a group of colleagues agree. They agree to understand reality in a certain way. When somebody comes along who violates that agreement, irrespective of the dimensions of his unique message, he is regarded as an oddball. From Archimedes to Copernicus, from bloodletting to acupuncture, from the search for an infinite God to the search for a cure for cancer, the history of science is a history of oddballs clashing with the significant idols of the day.

But this is not a book about science. This is a book about oddballs. Science just happens to be one of the many arenas in which the struggle for individualization takes place. We are here interested in science to the extent that it can help illuminate our study of the relationships between the individualizing self and the social group that forms the context for human individuality. To this end, we shall study a few oddballs from a particular science, the science of human behavior and human personality, more commonly known as psychology. Psychology as a distinct scientific discipline has a briefer history than most sciences, a fact that will allow us to trace its history of idols and oddballs in a fairly succinct fashion. Nor is there any shortage of oddballs in the history of psychology!

The standard textbooks on the history of psychology would have us believe that psychology had its beginning in the most auspicious of scientific circumstances. Tales are told to the effect that psychology had its inceptions in the tight little laboratories of constipated German professors late in the nineteenth century. In this textbook account, dedicated searchers for the data of truth, like Wilhelm Wundt, burned midnight oil night after night in the attempt to achieve an objective, experimental description of human behavior. This view, in my opinion, attempts to promote the notion that the science of psychology is a value-free enterprise, which is able to achieve an objective set of canons and conventions that lead to the real truth about human nature. This is a view worth balancing, I think, with some input from some of the magnificent oddballs who have walked the way of psychological science.

Let us turn back the clock of time, back to the days when there were giants upon the earth. Back to the days before the advent of the psychological laboratory, when inventive men and women waxed glibly about the nature of human existence without fear of being challenged by some compulsive scientist's myopic vision and piecemeal bank of experimental data. Back to the days of the bold stroke, when research was a way of scanning the horizon rather than meticulously plotting the underbelly of the beetle. Back to the days of prescientific psychology, when the madness for phrenology had "seized the tiller of the world," as Teilhard de Chardin would put it. For the real beginnings of psychology, psychiatry, social work, and the kindred disciplines are to be found in the totally bizarre and long-gone enterprise that was known as phrenology.

The term *phrenology* is derived from the Greek equivalents that mean "the study of mind." In the 22nd edition of *Stedman's Medical Dictionary*, it still receives a passing notation: "An obsolete doctrine, according to which each of the mental faculties is located in a definite part of the cerebral cortex, the size of which part varies in a direct ratio with the development of the corresponding faculty, this size being indicated by the external configuration of the skull."[1] The phrase "an obsolete doctrine" hides, I think, a host of meanings and covers a multitude of sins.

Phrenology was first formulated as an organized point of view by the Viennese physician, Dr. Franz Joseph Gall, near the turn of the nineteenth century. Gall, throughout his medical career, had been fascinated by the anatomy and physiology of the brain and had long toyed with the notion that a person's character, abilities, and social dispositions—in fact, the whole of the human personality—might well be related in a simple and direct fashion to the shape of the person's head. In time, Gall's hypothesis of concomitance between man's mind and his cranium began taking clearer form and perspective. Gall began to theorize that the brain is the organ of the mind in the same way that the eye is the organ of sight and that the ear is the organ of hearing; he began to assume that the structures of the brain and its encasing skull must surely correspond to the faculties and traits of human character. His theorizing led him to conclude that for every trait of human character—intelligence, memory, agreeableness, amativeness (sexuality), adhesiveness (love of friends), etc.—there must be a corresponding area of the brain and the encasing skull which increases in physical size in relation to the development of that particular faculty in any particular person. (Imagine! An organ for oddballlitry!) In order to read a man's character, one would simply analyze the bumps on his skull and contours of his cranium.

It should be emphasized that Gall was not a quack by any stretch of the term. He was an eminent and respected physician-scientist who pursued a lifelong interest in the anatomy of the brain and did so according to the scientific canons of his era. Standard medical histories continue to credit him for his scientific contributions to the understanding of localization of brain function and cerebral processes as well as his demonstration of the fibers of the medulla and the decussation of the pyramids of the brain.[2] Gall, courageously or foolishly, took a step beyond brain anatomy, however, in the interests of developing a more comprehensive view. His hypothesis that it was possible to diagnose and determine accurately the intellectual, social, and moral qualities of an individual by the inspection and palpation of the skull found many enthusiastic supporters. It also incurred the wrath of the establishment. It seemed that Gall's position apparently involved a denial of the existence of the soul and on that count was condemned both by the emperor and ecclesiastical authorities as well. Dr. Gall's "materialistic" views succeeded in prompting the authorities to insist on his departure from Vienna in 1805, and in collaboration with his most passionate supporter, Johann Gaspar Spurzheim, he lectured throughout Europe for some twenty years. In the process, he became a celebrity of considerable proportions, gathered an enthusiastic following of partisan supporters, and sufficiently advertised the doctrine of phrenology so that it became all the rage.

When Gall died in 1828, he passed the mantle of phrenology on to his disciple Spurzheim, who in 1832 made a lecture tour of the United States. This new science of phrenology would prove to be especially suited to a new nation filled with the pioneer spirit. Spurzheim's reception in the United States was phenomenal. Ralph Waldo Emerson, the eminent poet and essayist, flatly dubbed Spurzheim "one of the world's greatest minds," but, in the midst of his American lecture tour, Spurzheim suddenly and unexpectedly died, only to have his own brain preserved in alcohol in the laboratory of the Harvard Medical School.[3] And yet, the American climate was right for the science and practice of phrenology, and Spurzheim's untimely death would prove to be extremely timely for the launching of this new science of man. As Madeleine Stern notes in her marvelous book *Heads & Headlines*, the science of phrenology would give "to the country a practical answer to the Sphinx's question, What is man?"[4]

The attempt to define the riddle of the Sphinx in the practical language of the phrenological science was carried to its outer limits by two marvelously oddball brothers and one oddball sister, Orson, Lorenzo, and Charlotte Fowler. The Fowlers three were the offspring of pioneer stock, and one of their ancestors, known as the Giant of America, was reputed to have collared a five hundred pound shark, shouldered it in the shallows, and carried it huffing and puffing onto the shore. The task of the younger Fowlers was no less formidable, for they were destined to carry the message of phrenology to an unbelieving and scoffing populace.

Orson, the oldest and most outspoken, was clearly the leader of the new scientific cult. He had been a student at Amherst College when Spurzheim had ventured to America, and his intellectual conversion to phrenology was rapid and complete. By the time of his graduation from Amherst, Orson Fowler was well-versed in the science of the human faculties as well as the actual "feeling up" of the human skull. As a student, young Orson had taken to examining the skulls and predicting the characterological strengths and weaknesses of anyone and everyone who would allow him to get his eager hands on their knotty little gourds.

Orson Fowler's professional life began soon after he had completed his education at Amherst. He had intended to study for the ministry at Lane Seminary, but decided to eschew the orthodox pulpit for the unorthodox practice of analyzing human character from the configuration of the skull. Orson Fowler was in fact a veritable wizard at the instantaneous analysis of a person's character, whereas his younger brother Lorenzo was more gifted in the matter-of-fact teaching of phrenological hypotheses. Their combined talents in the practice of phrenology were considerable and more than equal to the task of taking phrenology to the grass-roots of America.   With a sure sense of dedication and purpose, the fabulous Fowlers took to the road, the ever-increasing audiences of the nineteenth-century lecture circuit, in order to demonstrate and defend the integrity and utility of the new science.

In the hands of the Fowlers, phrenology was as measured a science of man as had ever been known. They were not mystics and they were not charlatans. They were not selling patent medicines or hawking nostrums. Their intent was to make known this new science so that people could understand themselves in a scientific fashion. At a typical lecture, they would present the basic dicta and assumptions of phrenology in a straightforward manner and then proceed to invite members of the audience to the rostrum for an applied demonstration. When one or several members of the audience had volunteered, the Fowlers would then proceed with the phrenological examination of the subject in a highly methodical fashion. As Madeleine Stern notes:

> Even before they had examined a skull, the brothers had gauged the temperament of their subject. Size was their next point of interest; to determine this, they measured the horizontal circumference of the head with a tape. Form too was significant; placing their hands upon the sides of the subject's head, they investigated its shape. With one hand on the forehead and the other on the "basilar portion," they proceeded to study the relative developments of those regions. Applying the balls of their fingers, they moved the scalp slightly, becoming thoroughly familiar with the head they were examining. They rarely looked for bumps—although their work would so often be denigrated as "bumpology."
>
> Having determined the general size and shape of the skull, they proceeded to more specific areas, investigating the individual organs or faculties. Since the organ of Amativeness, for example, occupied the cerebellum at the base of the back part of the head, the Fowlers to explore it, felt along the middle line toward the base of the skull. There, below a small bony projection called the occipital process, behind the bottom of the ears, lay the sought-for organ of Amativeness. Having found it, they determined its size, designated by numbers from 1 to 7. If the organ was extremely small—1, 2, or 3—it required cultivation; if it was inordinately large—7—it required control and repression. The earliest charts, marking the various faculties by size, were in great demand by the subject, who, intent upon knowing himself, could contemplate the size or power of his Combativeness, Destructiveness, his Firmness and

Ideality, his Acquisitiveness and Cautiousness. As they manipulated, the Fowlers talked; their language, racy and vivid, painted character in broad strokes . . . . As they practiced, their fingers became twenty feelers and they themselves "two wizards of manipulation" who could "take a man's character right out from his keeping and hold it up before a whole meeting-house full of folks."[5]

Nor did the clients of the phrenological Fowlers allow them to practice without stern tests of their metier. Contemporary science allows the scientist to test his hypotheses in the privacy of his laboratory and holds him only to a public discussion of his findings in the appropriate scientific journals. The Fowlers, on the other hand, were required to show everything in the direct sight of the public. In order to test the credibility of this new science, the public demanded that the Fowlers perform their examinations blindfolded or even doubly blindfolded. One of the Fowlers would be led blindfolded from the stage to a room outside of hearing range, while the other would examine a subject while wearing a blindfold; the two brothers would then be required to reverse the roles and the previously secluded brother would be required to analyze the same client who had been examined previously in full public view. The audiences would rig other tests for the unsuspecting Fowlers. Occasionally a clergyman would disguise himself in the clothing of a commercial drummer and approach the stage with a rudeness of language and a frivolous manner, all intended to mislead the phrenologist and to test the accuracy of his analyses.[6]

The intent of the phrenologist, of course, was more than showmanship. By the scientific analysis of the individual character, it was presumed that personality strengths and weaknesses could be clearly defined so that the person could cope more effectively with the management of his life. Phrenology was a form of self-knowledge that could thus enable a person to understand himself more appropriately and to plan his life accordingly. For example, Lorenzo Fowler once examined a fifteen-year-old girl in the town of Oxford, Massachusetts, whose parents were troubled by the child's shy withdrawn behavior. Fowler's examination revealed a sensitivity of nature, which he felt could never be outgrown. He predicted that "she will never assert herself for herself—she will suffer wrong first—but for others she will be perfectly fearless."[7] His advice to the parents was to throw responsibility on the little girl, which the parents did gladly, pleased as they were to have a strategy by which to raise their daughter. The young woman was Clara Barton, who grew up to be the founder of the American Red Cross! What contemporary psychiatrist or psychologist could claim such remarkable results from a single intervention!

The Fowlers' skills in the science and practice of phrenology in time earned them the respect and recognition of men of substance in American life. Orson, for example, was asked to read the skull of the future president of the United States, then Senator John Tyler, in whom he found such considerable faculties of Self-esteem and Firmness that he described Tyler as a man who "would veto bills." Horace Mann, the eminent educator, became a devoted advocate, as did Horace Greeley who regularly supported the new science with editorials in his *Tribune*. Henry Ward Beecher, the famed Unitarian minister, preached the reliability of the new science from his considerable pulpit in Brooklyn's Plymouth Church. Perhaps, the most noteworthy accomplishment of the still young science, however, was a charting done by Lorenzo Fowler on July 16, 1849. The skull read by the younger Fowler on that particular day was that of one W. Whitman, aged twenty-nine, an unknown printer. The skull belonged, of course, to Walt Whitman who would soon establish himself as one of America's most accomplished poets. Fowler read Whitman's head and then dictated the following character analysis to his secretary to be preserved in handwritten form for the young printer-poet:

You were blessed by nature with a good constitution and power to live to a good old age. You were undoubtedly descended from a long-lived family. You were not (like many) prematurely developed—did not get ripe like a hot house-plant but you can last long and grow better as you grow older if you are careful to obey the laws of health, of life, and of mental and physical development. You have a large sized brain giving you much mentality as a whole. You are well calculated to enjoy social life— Few men have all the social feelings as strong as you have. Your love and regard for woman as such are strong and you are for elevating and ameliorating the female character. You were inclined to marry at an early age. You could not well bear to be deprived of you[r] domestic privileges and enjoyments. You are very fond of children or pets and would much desire to have your own intelligent and respected. You are also very fond of home and think much of having one of your own and of making it comfortable and attractive. You would like to travel and yet to go and leave family and friends would be a task. You are one of the most friendly men in the world and your happiness is greatly depending on your social relations. You are familiar and open in your intercourse with others but you do not by so doing lose your dignity. You would be or are a kind husband—an affectionate father and a sincere friend and a feeling obliging neighbor. You can easily pass from one thing to another and you prefer short comprehensive speeches to long yarns about nothing. You have much energy when you are aroused but you are not easily moved at trifles. You would if obliged to, fight bravely for friends, woman, moral character, children and honor. You choose to fight with tongue and pen rather than with your fist. You are not quarrelsome but you mind your own business and like to see others do the same. You are cautious and look well to the future to consequences and obstructions and are generally pretty sure you are right before you "go ahead." Your courage is probably more moral than physical. Your appetite is most too strong naturally and your food relishes well. You are pretty well calculated to resist disease and to soon recover if you are attacked by it. You are no hypocrite but are plain spoken and are what you appear to be at all times. You are in fact most too open at times and have not alway[s] enough restraint in speech. You are more careful about what you do than you are about what you say—You are independent, not wishing to be a slave yourself or to enslave others. You have your own opinions and think for yourself. You wish to work on your own hook, and are inclined to take the lead. You are very firm in general and not easily driven from your position. Your sense of justice, of right and wrong is strong and you can see much that is unjust and inhuman in the present condition of society. You are but little inclined to the spiritual or devotional and have but little regard for creeds or ceremonies. You are not any too sanguine and generally realize as much as you hope for—You are very sympathetic and easily moved by suffering and take much interest in those movements that are of a reformatory and philanthropic character. You are not any too fond of property but value it as a means—are not a penny-man, and despise narrowminded penuriousness—You have taste and considerable imagination but it does not blind you to fact or reality. You can adapt yourself to time place and company but you do not try to act out another's character but are yourself at all times. You have both reason and perception and hence can reason well. You have a strong desire to see everything and your knowledge is practical and available. You have a good mechanical eye and can judge well of and recollect forms and proportions well. You have a good sense of order either mentally or physically. By practice might make a good accountant. You can locate well and have a taste for geography. You are a great reader and have a good memory of facts and events much better than their time. You can compare, illustrate, discriminate, and criticise with much ability. You can be sarcastic if you choose. You are a good physiognomist. You have a good command of language especially if excited.[8]

Whitman himself was very much taken by this penetrating analysis of his skull and personality. Several editions of *Leaves of Grass*, Whitman's most famous and accomplished work, would bear the following phrenological chart as described by Fowler:

This man has a grand physical constitution, and power to live to a good old age. He is undoubtedly descended from the soundest and hardiest stock. Size of head large. Leading traits of character appear to be Friendship, Sympathy, Sublimity and Self-Esteem, and markedly among his combinations the dangerous faults of Indolence, a tendency to the pleasure of Voluptuousness and alimentiveness, and a certain reckless swing of animal will, too unmindful, probably, of the conviction of others.

Amativeness large 6, Philoprogenitiveness 6, Adhesiveness 6, Inhabitiveness 6, Concentrativeness 4, Combativeness 6, Destructiveness 5 to 6, Alimentiveness 6, Acquisitiveness 4, Secretiveness 3, Cautiousness 6, Approbativeness 4, Self-Esteem 6 to 7, Firmness 6 to 7, Conscientiousness 6, Hope 4, Marvellousness 3, Veneration 4, Benevolence 6 to 7, Constructiveness 5, Ideality 5 to 6, Sublimity 6 to 7, Imitation 5, Mirthfulness 5, Individuality 6, Form 6, Size 6, Weight 6, Color 3, Order 5, Calculation 5, Locality 6, Eventuality 6, Time 3, Tune 4, Language 5, Causality 5 to 6, Comparison 6, Suavitiveness 4, Intuitiveness, or Human Nature 6.[9]

Whitman was proud of his phrenological features, and in many respects *Leaves of Grass* is simply a poetic affirmation of belief in the new science, its major themes involving the notions of the perfectability of human nature and the improvability of the human condition.

Phrenology in the hands of the Fowlers was *the* signal human science of the mid-nineteenth century. The Fowler family and their associates would come to publish a host of scientific books and journals, not the least of which were Orson Fowler's: (1) *Love and Parentage, Applied to the Improvement of Offspring; a Phrenological Guide* (a very sensible book on child-rearing), (2) *Creative and Sexual Science* (written in 1870 when Freud was only fourteen years old, and filled with avant-garde ideas and suggestions in the psychology of sexuality, including many how-to-do-it promptings), and (3) *Human Science or Phrenology* (a basic textbook in nineteenth century psychology).

Creative and Sexual Science, for example, was a wondrously direct and human statement of the nature of human sexuality, in an age that was not especially liberated in that regard. Orson Fowler candidly championed full sexual enjoyment for both partners and proclaimed himself an advocate of full breasts, a well-formed pubis, and *summum bonum* enjoyment of coitus. His book is filled with astounding utterances, such as, "Men undersized, but highly electric, are far better than those large, yet stag-like," and "Well-sexed women set their breasts forward . . . by carrying their shoulders clear back as far as possible." Fowler saw his book as a basic statement of phrenology and sexual hygiene, and his avowed purpose was to teach all. In his own words, "This Book Nails Its Flag Fast. It may be killed, but it don't surrender. It proffers sexual knowledge to old and young, married and single, maidens included, and defies all its opponents to their teeth."[10] Shades of Drs. Freud, Kinsey, and Masters!

The Fowlers were oddballs, armed to the teeth in the tenets of their new science, and willing and able to take on all scoffers and infidels. Nor can there be any question that their mutual and respective accomplishments were considerable, and this despite the fact that their "science" was based on some fairly squirrelly assumptions. The canons of science in the mid-nineteenth century were, of course, considerably different from contemporary notions about "good science."

By contemporary standards, phrenology would be found deficient because its exponents never performed the kind of careful experimental analysis that has come to be the rule-of-thumb for acceptable scientific procedure. Yet, the Fowlers certainly were not charlatans. They were always eager to place everything that they did squarely before the public, and they regularly entertained all sorts of public challenges to their scientific beliefs and practices. If contemporary human scientists were asked to defend their findings and their assumptions in the manner of an Orson Fowler, they would likely wilt beneath the heat of public opinion.

What are we to think of this "science" of phrenology which ruled the psychological thought of a century now past? Is it more akin to the reading of tea leaves than to the scientific study of human personality? Is it merely a discredited pseudo-science left by the inevitable tides of scientific progress? Or does phrenology teach us something about the nature of science in any age, including our own?

Contemporary human scientists have great difficulty accepting the basic assumptions of phrenology. They cite the lack of any demonstrable relationship between the contours of the brain and the contours of the skull. They cite the lack of any proven relationship between the size of particular global areas of the brain and the concomitant possession of general characteristics of personality and/or moral character. Without evidence in support of these assumptions, it would seem that the entire superstructure of phrenology is doomed to crumble.

And yet, when contemporary human scientists allow themselves to be excruciatingly honest about modern scientific data, they are hard put to find any judgment about human personality which receives sufficient scientific support to be credibly delivered into the annals of "real truth." No science is expected to "prove" its assumptions but only to articulate its point of view and to conduct research that tends to flow from the point of view set forth. There is no truth in science except that value which is given to an idea or a finding by a community of believers who hold the finding to be relevant and consistent to a particular set of principles.

Phrenology has not been discredited, although it has grown obsolete. It has lost its champions, and men of conviction and dedication have gone on to other postulates and other scientific views. The oddball Fowlers who gave impetus to this passing understanding of man's nature have given way to other oddballs who have forged different paths and alternate routes throughout the maze of human understanding and experience. As Madeleine Stern observed:

> The thinking man of the "Wonderful Century" has placed his burnt offerings on the altar of the laboratory table, poured his libations into the test tube, and, with seeming finality, shattered that nineteenth-century image of man—the phrenological head . . . . Yet for those with eyes to see the past recur in the present, that head emerges now and again whole, unbroken, with all its faculties marked, bearing its implicit message of perfectability, pointing the way to reform. The work of the Fowler brothers lingers on, albeit intermittently and in strange places.[11]

As we proceed in this study of oddballs, of men who believe in themselves and in the power of their beliefs and convictions, we will pass to the study of that unique individual who singlehandedly posited the maxims for the study of man in the first half of the twentieth century. In the oddball character of Sigmund Freud and his own science of psychoanalysis, there will be considerable cause to compare Fowlerian phrenology and Freudian psychoanalysis. As Karl M. Dallenbach has written in the *American Journal of Psychology*, "Despite their separation in time of 100 years, they are so similar that Psychoanalysis is almost a case of history repeating itself . . . for though the voice and the words are new—the structure, form and development of refrain are those of Phrenology."[12]

The phrenological Fowlers were genuine oddballs precisely because of their ability to champion a unique point of view in the science of man. They sought a way to test man's understanding of himself by stepping beyond the common beliefs and by vigorously attending to their own convictions. In their own day they were thought to be quite odd, and the scientist as well as the man-in-the-street found their oddball science to be quite upsetting. Phrenology is no longer fashionable, but it has not been disproven. As a chapter in the history of human science, it is frequently overlooked. And yet, I believe that we must still ask ourselves whether the science of our day is any better. Is there anything that renders one form of science better than another form of science? Isn't it all a matter of convention?

12 Sigmund Freud

Psychoanalysis and the Science of the "Un"

SIGMUND FREUD (1856-1939) has long been reclassified. In the current annals and histories of the human sciences, Freud is now recognized as a founding father, a patriarch, a tradition-maker, a giant of a thinker whose vision stands as an illuminating beacon across the darkness of the human condition. Although Freud's approach to the science of human personality continues to elicit more than its fair share of attackers and detractors, his pre-eminence in the field of the human sciences is unquestioned. Whether one sees in Sigmund Freud a hero to be deified or a demon to be exorcized, his thinking nonetheless represents one of the major contributions to the evolution of twentieth century thought. Freud has become a frame of reference, an intellectual backdrop, a commanding point of view against which new ideas are compared and evaluated. In a few short years, Freudianism has become the conventional wisdom of the intellectual marketplace.

167

Freud's transmogrification to the realm of the gods and patriarchs (or, depending on your point of view, to the realm of the devil and his henchman) is especially fitting when we consider the intense opposition and meagerness of recognition that were accorded to him early in his career. Sigmund Freud did not start out as the Father of Psychoanalysis, nor were his ideas received with any degree of enthusiasm in the early days of this century. I say this with the intention of whimsical understatement. This Viennese physician who is now recognized as one of the greatest minds of modern times began his career as an oddball in the classic style. As a matter of fact, the main thrust of his most significant contributions continues to run counter to mankind's most basic beliefs about itself. Although Freudianism has become respectable and even widely accepted in certain intellectual circles, there is no doubt—in my mind at least—that most people who would be given a fair hearing of Freud's basic ideas would likely reject the notions as the ravings of a madman.

As Lenny Bruce was wont to observe, "Publicity is stronger than sanity!" Freudianism has been sufficiently publicized that even the ill-educated layman has some form of nodding knowledgeability of Freud. Freudianism has been in the air long enough that most people tend to maintain their aplomb in discussing psychoanalysis as a form of psychological treatment, a theory of personality, or a philosophy of human nature. Despite its increasing acceptability as a science of human personality, however, the fundamentals of psychoanalytic doctrine remain alarmingly offbeat ideas to which the great majority of mankind would have considerable difficulty lending their allegiance. The controversial nature of psychoanalysis is due, in my opinion, to the frankly oddball leanings of its founder, the eminent Dr. Freud.

The life and ideas of Sigmund Freud are still close enough to the heartbeat of contemporary man and the tempo of current times that it is difficult to separate Freud from the movement that followed him. Sigmund Freud and Freudianism are not necessarily horses of the same color. In my own professional life, I have had the pleasure and the displeasure of rubbing elbows with a goodly number of believing Freudians. In the main, the balance swings significantly in the direction of displeasure. To be painfully candid in this matter, Freudianism as a movement seems to have fostered or attracted more than its fair share of pompous autocrats who wax authoritative on every issue under the sun. In the hands of lesser men, psychoanalysis seems all too easily to lend itself to illusions of omniscience and infallibility. Such, at least, has been the experience of this writer.

Independent of one's attitudes toward the personalities of the practitioners, however, psychoanalysis has achieved the distinction of a unique science of human personality. There are many, of course, who would maintain that referring to psychoanalysis as a science is merely a way of gilding the lily. The eminent and highly regarded behavioral scientist Robert Sears, for example, has referred to psychoanalysis as "a finely etched grotesquerie," an observation hardly intended to rhapsodize the scientific merits of the psychoanalytic enterprise. Most tough-minded behavioral scientists are provoked to fits of laughter or mouthings of contempt whenever psychoanalysis is extolled as a science. But that's the problem of the tough-minded behavioral scientists. The fact remains that psychoanalysts by and large regard themselves as practitioners of science and they have had considerable success in convincing many of their professional and scientific colleagues to adopt a similar viewpoint.

And yet, psychoanalysis is a very unusual science. Its major public forum, the International Psychoanalytic Association, was founded with the avowed intention to ". . . foster and further the science of psychoanalysis founded by Freud, both as a pure discipline of psychology and in its application to medicine and the mental sciences . . . ."[1] The goal of this association was primarily to further the science *founded by*

Freud. We would be remiss in failing to point out that the International Psychoanalytic Association was itself founded by Freud. The Association, founded by Freud, was founded by Freud with the intention of fostering a science founded by Freud, which incidentally was founded by Freud. This Freud was an unusual man who founded an unusual science. Biologists, for example, do not study evolution as founded by Darwin, even though Darwin is unquestionably the founding father of biological evolutionism. What webs does he weave, this Sigmund Freud? And what kind of man founds his own science as well as an association to keep it pure?

The simple truth, by his own admission, is that Freud was an adventurer in the world of ideas. In a letter to a colleague, written in February, 1900, long before Freud had achieved any significant notoriety, he gingerly observed:

> You often estimate me too highly. For I am not really a man of science, not an observer, not an experimenter, and not a thinker. I am nothing but by temperament a *conquistador*—an adventurer, if you want to translate the word—with the curiosity, the boldness, and the tenacity that belong to that type of being. Such people are apt to be treasured if they succeed, if they have really discovered something; otherwise they are thrown aside. And that is not altogether unjust.[2]

Later that same year, Freud further revealed himself to that same friend:

> No critic, not even the stupid Loewenfeld, the Burchkardt of Neuropathology, can see more keenly than I do the disproportion between the problems and the solutions, and I shall suffer the just punishment that none of the undiscovered provinces of mental life which I was the first mortal to enter will bear my name or follow the laws I have formulated.[3]

Freud did not see himself as discovering laws but rather as formulating them. He did not see himself as a poor, benighted scientist, humbled before the mysteries of life.

Freud was not in the business of merely trying to find suitable expressions that would clarify the datum of his clinical observations. Rather, he was searching for the grand idea, the magnificent rationale, the integrating point of view that would provide a total understanding of the human condition. He *was* an adventurer, and his adventure was the attempt to provide a kaleidoscopic view of human personality and human society, in all of their manifold ramifications.

In his early work as a neurologist, Freud was constantly faced with the fact that neurology was singularly lacking an adequate rationale to explain either normal behavior or pathological conditions. The "science" of phrenology, of course, had achieved a marvelous theoretical synthesis between the brain and behavior. Gall, Spurzheim, and the Fowlers had maintained that the behaviors associated with human character must surely "exercise" relevant areas of the brain producing corresponding bumps in the human skull. The whole notion seemed perfectly plausible on paper, and in the hands of the fabulous Fowlers occasionally achieved heights of clinical intuition and practical genius. But phrenology had proved useless to the serious scientist and conventional healer. The field of neurology and psychiatry was rapidly evolving, and there was increasing need for a comprehensive theory and method of treatment to guide the laboratory investigations of serious scientists as well as the clinical exigencies of medical practice. Freud sensed the need for the bold stroke.

Freud's bold stroke, his grand idea that would lay bare the manifold complexities and hidden secrets of human behavior in all of its dynamic dimensions, did not seize him in sudden moment. No clouds opened up, no doves descended. Nothing miraculous. Freud toiled long and hard, sometimes seeing patients as many as twelve to fourteen hours a day, and then burned the midnight oil, recording his ideas, sifting the wheat from the chaff, gradually venturing into print, at first with little notice but gradually with an increasingly negative reception. In 1900, for example, Freud published

The Interpretation of Dreams, a book that is now regarded as a classic. At the time of its publication, it made scarcely a ripple in the psychological stream. Ernest Jones, Freud's biographer, notes that the then-noted psychologist Wilhelm Stern observed that the only effect of the book would be that "uncritical minds would be delighted to join in this play with ideas and would end up in complete mysticism and chaotic arbitrariness."[4] The initial reaction to Freud's early work was to dismiss it as a joke. Freud, however, had not as yet achieved a sufficiently bold stroke. Throughout the first decade of the twentieth century, he continued to winnow and refine his notions about human behavior. Little by little and step by step, Freud was coming ever closer to a stunning insight about the human condition: in both the prosaic as well as the significant aspects of human life, *most people do not know why they do what they do but Sigmund Freud does know*! Freud, the adventurer in ideas, had consummately one-upped the human race. Because of his unique discovery, a discovery that would secure his lasting fame, Freud would be able to know things about people that they could not possibly know about themselves. Freud had discovered "the dynamic unconscious."

As early as 1897, Freud had written that "the unconscious is the true psychical reality; in its inner nature it is just as unknown to us as is the reality of the outer world, and it is just as imperfectly communicated to us by the data of consciousness as is the outer world through the information reaching us from our sense organs."[5] The notion of an "unconscious mind" in man, of course, was not unique to Sigmund Freud. Many of his predecessors and contemporaries theorized and grappled with the problem of an unconscious aspect to man's behavior and brain functioning. And yet, Freud alone had come to the conclusion of a *dynamic unconscious*, a set of mental processes within the individual that influence and exert control over behavior, thoughts, and feelings that are present at the conscious level and seemingly under the conscious control of the individual.

Freud's postulation of a dynamic unconscious shattered the age-old conception of man as an independent master of his fate. As David Stafford-Clark has observed:

> The analogy of the iceberg has sometimes been used to remind us that the unconscious area of mental life is vastly greater than the conscious or consciously remembered areas. If everything that we know and remember is regarded as the part of the iceberg above the surface, at least seven times as much lies below the surface, and determines both the centre of gravity of the whole, and much of the movements, direction and fate of the iceberg.[6]

Freud's unconscious is an active, unknown force, determining man's behavior and exerting tremendous power over man's ability to direct his behavior.

Freud's "discovery" of the unconscious was, of course, ill-received and roundly criticized. Reuben Fine, in his otherwise excellent commentary, seems to think that Freud himself was unconscious of the implications of this doctrine:

> The idea of an unconscious mind was fought with the most incredible arguments by Freud's colleagues. *As he later came to realize* [italics mine], he had dealt the world a severe blow; in effect, what he said to men was that they were not really masters in their own house. All of a sudden, the facade behind which they assure themselves that they were aware of all their motives collapsed, and it is understandable that such a shock should be ardently fought.[7]

As he later came to realize? Dr. Fine would have us believe that Dr. Freud really didn't understand what he was doing in fostering the view of a dynamic unconscious motivating man's behavior. According to Fine's perspective, Freud is portrayed as some sort of guiltless altar boy innocently draining off the vicar's supply of altar wine in the interests of a well-intentioned curiosity about the meaning of the mass. I don't think so. I don't think that Freud's motivations were all that unconscious. I don't think that Freud was innocent of the realization that his theory was a means of distinguishing himself from his colleagues, while at the same time lifting his index finger in the time-honored means of saluting the establishment.

Throughout his life, Freud was absolutely delighted with the fact that he had discovered a genuinely different way of viewing human existence, and he luxuriated in the feeling associated with his novel insights. In 1932, Freud composed a special preface to the English edition of *The Interpretation of Dreams*, the publication which had limned his theory of the dynamic unconscious some thirty-two years previous. In that preface he wrote:

> This book, with the new contribution to psychology which *surprised the world* [italics mine] when it was published (1900), remains essentially unaltered. It contains, even according to my present-day judgment, the most valuable of all the discoveries which it has been my good fortune to make. Insight such as this falls to one's lot but once in a lifetime.[8]

Freud loved it! (It should be noted, by the way, that this book hardly surprised the world when it was first published. The initial printing of six hundred copies took eight years to sell. Freud received the princely sum of $209 in royalties for this first edition. Perhaps, he had reason to want to rub it in a little!)

Moreover, Freud's interest in evolving a strikingly novel view of human behavior was not merely a passing fancy that might be attributed to the vagaries of his youth. His investment in oddballlitry was lifelong and life-consuming. Having discovered the nature of the dynamic unconscious, Freud evolved all sorts of unusual ideas about the contents of the unconscious processes which he had postulated were the inner core of man's existence as well as the foundations of human society. Throughout his life, Freud continued to stun the medical and scientific establishment with highly unique and universally upsetting statements about the true nature of man's inner self. The discovery of the unconscious was just the beginning.

Freud had achieved a view from within. His postulation of unconscious processes lurking beneath the disguise of conscious control allowed him to lift the veil which hid man's supposedly truer countenance. His professional practice had come to focus exclusively on the technique of psychoanalysis, and in patient after patient he sought to move beyond the simple presenting concerns which clients brought to him. Through dream analysis, free association, and sensitive listening, he became increasingly aware of the complex ways in which overt symptoms were merely the signals of repressed, unconscious conflicts. The more he saw of the inner, hidden working of unconscious mind, the more he became convinced that the nature of psychological conflicts involved clearly sexual factors. As Ernest Jones has pointed out:

> *To his own great surprise* [italics mine], and against his personal puritanical predilections, Freud was finding himself more and more compelled by the results of his investigations to attach importance to the sexual factors in aetiology . . . . It was no sudden discovery, and—in spite of what his opponents have suggested—it was quite unconnected with any preconceptions. Only very gradually, and—as it seems to us now—slowly, did Freud become convinced of the significance of sexual factors and of the extensive part they play in buried mental life. The importance of sexuality in early childhood, and its essentially incestuous nature, ideas which brought down such a storm on his head, he learned of in a curiously inverse way. He at first accepted his patients' stories of their parents' sexual overtures toward them when they were children, but came to realize that the stories were simply phantasies derived from his patients' own childhood.[9]

To his own great surprise? Freud's biographers would have us believe that he was some sort of nincompoop, living in a state of constant amazement or regularly reeling with shock. He may not have been a simple wild-eyed revolutionary hellbent on "upping" the establishment, but he knew what he was doing. Freud was finding out about his clients' sexual lives and fantasies because he was asking and not because his clients were thrusting their libidos at him against his will. Most assuredly, Freud was a serious investigator, compelled to articulate his observations irrespective of the consequences. The consequences were, of course, considerable, not the least of which was the simple fact that friend after friend proceeded to abandon him because of his evolving view of the sexual nature of personal problems. And yet, Freud held fast to his convictions with a fierceness of spirit and independence of mind that have been rarely, if ever, equaled in the annals of human accomplishment. He would pursue his solitary vision, no matter what the cost. In the words of his chief biographer, "Freud developed or consolidated an attitude of mind that was to remain one of his most distinctive characteristics: an independence of other people's opinion. He had learned to stand alone in the world. . . . "[10]

The conclusions which Freud reached regarding the psychosexual nature of the human mind were, in fact, quite astounding. Even today in the far-out reaches of the emancipated seventies, Freud's views have fallen somewhat short of conventional acceptance. Sigmund Freud covered the innocence of human childhood with tar and feathers. The founder of psychoanalysis would let nothing stand in the way of his vision of the true nature of the human psyche, and he was far from loath to smash a few idols, including the purity of little kiddies. Freud and his followers have come to believe the most awful things about the minds and motivations of little children, awful, that is, from the standpoint of most conventional parents who are not overly eager to regard their little ones as ticking sex bombs. One of the most upsetting aspects of the analytic viewpoint involves the insistence that sexuality is not suddenly triggered at puberty but rather is present in the infant from birth. In *An Outline of Psychoanalysis*, Freud maintained:

> The first organ to emerge as an erotogenic zone and to make libidinal demands on the mind is, from the time of birth onwards, the mouth. To begin with, all psychical activity is concentrated on providing satisfaction for the needs of that zone. Primarily, of course, this satisfaction serves the purpose of self-preservation by means of nourishment; but physiology should not be confused with psychology. The baby's obstinate persistence in sucking gives evidence at an early age of a need for satisfaction which, though it originates from and is instigated by the taking of nourishment, nevertheless strives to obtain pleasure independently of nourishment, and for that reason may and should be termed *sexual*.[11]

One should note here that it would have been quite possible for Freud to make his point without insisting on the use of a term—namely, *sexual*—that could only be upsetting to his readers. Instead of "sexual," Freud could have used the terms "sensual" or "tactile" or whatever. But Freud always insisted on selecting the words that would strike directly at the resistances of his reading public and professional colleagues. He never backed off. Never. For example, in describing the compulsive personality, Freud coined the expression "anal character." There are easier ways of making the same point. In describing the growth crises of the female child, Freud evolved the term "penis envy," an expression that has been less than well-received by the current generation of feminists. Throughout his writings, the founder of psychoanalytic psychology regularly employed those expressions that would make his point with more than was necessary for crystal clarity.

Perhaps the most bothersome and unsettling

dimension of all Freudian theory is his designation of the Oedipus complex. Accepting the main lines of the Greek legend of *Oedipus Rex*, the tragic character who unknowingly killed his father and married his mother, Freud maintained that every child between the ages of four and six, roughly speaking, passes through an "Oedipal phase," in which the child wants to kill off the parent of the same sex and to enjoy sexual relations with the parent of the opposite sex. The specter of an army of libidinized little boys lusting hungrily after their mothers has been difficult for many sane observers to accept, and yet this doctrine remains one of the cardinal points of Freudian theory. Although the historical effects of the psychoanalytic movement have surely included a significant counterbalance to nineteenth-century puritanism—a counterbalance that is most noteworthy in the frank discussion of sexual matters and the emancipation of many areas of sexual behavior—one must still question why Freud found it necessary to state his views in such frankly pointed terminology. Freud undoubtedly must have believed that it was best to deal with the inevitable resistances to his ideas by means of the frontal attack, but according to the thesis advanced throughout this book he was also an oddball who had a singular investment in doing it his way.

Another area in which Freud enjoyed tweaking the nose of conventional wisdom was that of religion. In his personal life, Freud was an atheist who was openly antagonistic toward organized religion. As a psychoanalyst, Freud considered religion to be an infantile reaction, a kind of universal obsessional neurosis of mankind. It is again interesting to note that Freud chose to entitle his major work in this area *The Future of an Illusion*; failing to pull the punch, he opted to regard religion as an "illusion," another good term that had the effect of parading mankind's foolishness. Religious believers, in the Freudian view, are therefore doomed to acting at an infantile level in the pursuit of an illusion. Nor could Freud allow God to remain in his heaven. As I have written in another context,

In *Totem and Taboo*, Freud insinuates that the source of religion can be found in the sex drive, at least so far as the pervasive sense of guilt is a factor with which religion tries to cope. The guilt engendered by the failure to resolve the Oedipus complex results in an expression of tender feelings for the father and leads to the search for an adequate father image. It is out of this search that the idea of God arises. God is projected as an exalted father, and the longing for the father is the root of the need for religion.[12]

For Freud, religion was simply another false idol, a demeaning and growth-preventing complex buried unconsciously deep within man's inner life. Although his analysis of the religious sentiment and the idea of God was unquestionably quite offensive to the sensibilities of the devout, Freud, as usual, refused to allow any respect for social convention to interfere with his investigations and pronouncements. Such is the case with Freud's analysis of religion, with his theory of sexuality, and with almost every aspect of the psychoanalytic view. The science of psychoanalysis, in the hands of Freud, is a strikingly original and innovative method of viewing God, man, and the world. In many respects, Freud founded a "science" that would serve as a unique platform for the exposition of his own highly individualized understanding of reality.

To what can we attribute the fact that Sigmund Freud was able, indeed compelled, to evolve such a completely novel system of ideas and observations? Ernest Jones, in his monumental biography and excellent commentary, maintains that Freud's achievements were a direct function of his passionate thirst for truth: "Freud's passion to get at the truth with the maximum of certainty was, I again suggest, the deepest and strongest motive in his nature and the one that compelled him toward his pioneering achievements."[13] Consistent with the analytic viewpoint, Jones himself suggests that Freud's passion for truth was "fed by powerful motives arising in his infantile curiosity about the primary facts of life, the meaning of birth and what has brought it about."[14] These psychoanalysts are really screwed to their sticking places! Is Freud's lifelong passion to discover new things to be attributed to some childish curiosity about the sexual act that brought him into the world? I think not.

Erich Fromm, I think, offers a more compelling explanation of Freud's remarkable creativity. Fromm points out that Freud was a child of the enlightenment and that he fully embraced the enlightenment motto: *Sapere Aude*—Dare to know. For Fromm, Freud's accomplishments were made possible by his "uncompromising faith in reason."

> Reason, so Freud felt, is the only tool—or weapon—we have to make sense of life, to dispense with illusions (of which, in Freud's thought, religious tenets are only one), to become independent of fettering authorities, and thus to establish our own authority. This faith in reason was the basis for his relentless pursuit of the truth, once he had seen a theoretical truth in the complexity and manifoldness of observable phenomena. Even if results, from the standpoint of common sense, seemed to be absurd, this did not disturb Freud. On the contrary, the laughing mob, whose thinking was determined by the wish for convenience and an undisturbed sleep, only accentuated the difference between conviction and opinion, reason and common sense, truth and rationalization.[15]

Fromm further notes that Freud's father, who had been a rather prosperous manufacturer, had had to give up his business because of unexpected changes in the Austrian economy, a fact that made a considerable impression on the young Freud. "Freud as a young boy learned by drastic experience that social stability was to be as little trusted as political stability; that no tradition or conventional setup offered any security or deserved confidence."[16]

I do not think it is possible to achieve any sensible appreciation of Freud's mission to the world without seeing in him the awesome working of the dynamics of individuality.

Freud was completely independent of public opinion. With signal clarity, he once wrote to his disciple, Carl Jung, "Many enemies, much honor." Freud was determined to distinguish himself from his fellows, and the fact of opposition was merely a sign to him of his success. Even Jones finds solace in "Freud's determination to trust himself alone, to resist the impulse to believe others more than himself, and in this way to make imperishable the name of Freud."[17]

There is in the life and work of Sigmund Freud a marvelous lesson for mankind, a lesson that needs to be taught again and again. Freud knew that his age would resist him, but it made no difference. It was his own sense of his identity that really mattered. In this way, he was able to achieve a remarkable emancipation from human custom and a degree of individuality that few of us can come by. Although Freudian science may be a less than perfect affair, the lesson of his life remains.

In many ways, it is a sad shame that the Freudian heritage has been left in the hands of the psychoanalysts, a group that has become as schoolish and tradition-bound as any organized religion. The irony of it all is somehow not quite amusing. Freud, the man who shattered the illusions of his age, has left behind him yet another illusion, the illusion of the psychoanalytic movement and the host of new conventions it has fostered. The founder of psychoanalysis was much less orthodox in his approach to life and science than are the great majority of Freudians who have carried the doctrine of psychoanalysis to ridiculous extremes of orthodoxy and conventionality. What a terrible thing! To believe in Freud, rather than in oneself!

13 B.F. Skinner

The Anti-Autonomous Man

BURRHUS FREDERIC SKINNER—more commonly and for obvious reasons known as B. F. Skinner—has achieved the unique distinction of being America's most well-known social scientist. In a recent survey of highly visible scientists, Skinner was found to be considerably more recognizable than such scientific stalwarts as Jonas Salk (discoverer of the polio vaccine), Edward Teller (the physicist who engineered the atomic bomb), and Werner von Braun (the rocket expert whose wizardry propelled America to the moon).[1] Although Skinner's achievements in the behavioral sciences are many and considerable, it is unlikely that many members of the general public would be able to associate his name with any given discovery or achievement, as is the case with Salk, Teller, or von Braun. B. F. Skinner is a deviant.

A genuinely hard-core and tough-minded thinker, Skinner has probably done more to advance the scientific status of the behavioral disciplines than any other man. He is,

183

in fact, one of only three behavioral scientists who have ever received the president's Medal of Science, an honor that is usually reserved for outstanding accomplishment in the physical and biological sciences. In the behavioral sciences, Skinner's credentials and accomplishments are, indeed, without equal. A careful and creative laboratory experimenter, his systematic analyses of the behavior of laboratory organisms (chiefly rats and pigeons) stand as classics in the application of scientific method to the study of behavior. As early as 1931, as a Junior Fellow and recent Ph.D. at Harvard, Skinner began conducting extensive experiments on the relationship between the behavior of laboratory animals and various events within the environment that might influence the organism's behavior. It was in these early experiments that Skinner began to observe the orderly relationships that appeared to exist between behavior and the environmental events that follow upon a given behavior. In 1938, he presented an organized discussion and point of view of his laboratory investigations in his classic work *The Behavior of Organisms*.

The scientific themes advanced in this work, an approach that has subsequently come to be known as Skinnerian behaviorism, are that behavior is a function of its consequences and that a good deal of behavior is controlled by processes of *operant conditioning*. When laboratory animals are rewarded or reinforced for certain kinds of behaviors, they are more likely to repeat the performance of the behaviors in question. For example, if a rat presses a bar and is given a pellet of food, the rat is likely to press the bar again. Operant conditioning is simply the name for an observed process by which apparently spontaneous behaviors are strengthened and habituated when their occurrence is followed by a reinforcing event or reward within the environment. This is all fairly dull scientific stuff, and most of the material in *The Behavior of Organisms* could only catch the fancy of other behavioral scientists plying a similar trade.

From the purely scientific standpoint, the work was exceedingly careful, methodical, and well-controlled; it was "good science" but hardly the kind of thing that would stir men's minds. *The Behavior of Organisms*, however, was just a beginning. The real B. F. Skinner had not yet been counted. Nonetheless, the seeds of future directions were very much present in this early work, not the least of which was the clear recognition that behavior could be subject to systematic control.

Control, of course, is what B. F. Skinner is all about. All the while that Skinner was watching the rats and pigeons do their respective thing in his little laboratory boxes, he was thinking of bigger and better laboratories and more and more complex subjects. "Tomorrow the world" seems to have been the motto and secret dream of the young Skinner. In 1948, he published his utopian novel *Walden Two*, which is a straightforward platform for creating the perfect society in which all behavior is subject to the basic principles of operant conditioning. *Walden Two* is not about pigeons; rather, it is about people and the ways in which their behavior could be systematically controlled. The grand design had begun to emerge. B. F. Skinner had devised a plan for controlling the world and human destiny itself, all of which could be accomplished through the methodical application of scientific principles of behavior that he had discovered by giving pellets to pigeons. This is not a man who plays it close to the vest, despite the rigors of scientific training!

The plot and platform of *Walden Two* is advanced through the conversations of its two main characters, Burris and Frazier, both of whom are clearly Skinnerian alter egos. In a passage that has now grown famous, Skinner has Frazier lay out the basic issues:

> I have only one important characteristic, Burris: I'm stubborn. I've had only one idea in my life—a true *idee fixe* . . . to put it as bluntly as possible, the idea of having my own way. "Control" expresses it, I think. The

control of human behavior, Burris. In my early experimental days it was a frenzied, selfish desire to dominate.
I remember the rage I used to feel when a prediction
went awry. I could have shouted at the subjects of my
experiments, "Behave, damn you, behave as you
ought!"[2]

Control, indeed, is what B. F. Skinner is all about,
and it is his willingness, if not his outright eagerness, to
spell out the social implications of behavioral science that
renders him a genuine oddball.

Walden Two propelled Skinner out of the dim laboratories of academia and into the public spotlight. Although
this book was somewhat slow in catching on, it is now in its
umpteenth printing and has sold over a million copies.
(Skinner, consistent with his scientific spirit, is said to keep a
cumulative chart on his office wall plotting the monthly sales
of *Walden Two*.) Whereas many in the modern age have
feared the specter of an Orwellian 1984 when Big Brother
controls man's every thought and action, *Walden Two*
embraces and relishes the notion of a completely controlled
society. George Orwell felt that the completely controlled
society would be the ultimate hell; B. F. Skinner turns the
tables and maintains that the perfectly controlled society
would be the ultimate heaven. *Walden Two* is a projected
society in which all relevant human behavior is programmed
to run smoothly and efficiently by means of the Skinnerian
principles of operant conditioning.

This notion of a utopia controlled by the science of
behavior did not and does not sit well with the great majority
of Americans who have been bred on the sociopolitical philosophy of democratic idealism and all its many freedoms. The
response to *Walden Two* was sometimes articulate, often
vicious, and almost always negative. A good deal of *ad
hominem* criticism was directed squarely at Skinner himself,
the implication being that he was some sort of half-cocked
autocrat or mad would-be emperor. But Skinner never

balked. He never said, "Well, folks, I didn't really mean it that way." With impeccable aplomb, he continued to set forth, with an ever-increasing degree of articulation, that which he regarded to be the inevitable social implications and applications of behavioral science.

In a series of books and papers, Skinner has continued to define and refine the basic issues. In *Science and Human Behavior* (1953), an eminently readable volume, Skinner again posed the basic problem:

> Are we to continue to develop a science of behavior without regard to the use which will be made of it? If not, to whom is the control which it generates to be delegated?
>
> This is not only a puzzling question, it is a frightening one; for there is good reason to fear those who are most apt to seize control. To the suggestion that science would eventually be able "to control man's thoughts with precision" Winston Churchill once replied, "I shall be very content if my task in this world is done before that happens." This is not, however, a wholly satisfactory disposition of the problem.[3]

Skinner has appointed himself as mankind's conscience in this whole matter of science and behavioral control, and he will not let the issue go away. Perhaps his persistence in this matter is motivated by the concern that somebody might assume control of him. Whatever the source of his motivations, he has continued to emit a constant stream of public utterances that demonstrate a remarkable proclivity to raise the hackles of many other self-appointed guardians of the public trust.

By 1971, Skinner was ready for another bombshell. The publication of *Beyond Freedom and Dignity* was a signal event for the book reviewers of America. *Beyond Freedom* really touched off a storm of protest. For devout Skinner-watchers, the themes of *Beyond Freedom* began simply enough. "Twenty-five hundred years ago it might have been said that man understood himself as well as any other part of his world. Today he is the thing he understands least."[4] But Skinner understands, and he also understands the solutions to man's problems: "What we need is a technology of behavior."[5] These are old Skinner themes, but through the years Skinner had come to understand ever more clearly why people resisted the acceptance of a point of view which to him seemed obvious. The reason that people, even highly intelligent people, had resisted his proposed scientization of culture in which every human action would be carefully controlled was quite simple. Most people simply had misplaced values. They valued the wrong things. In *Beyond Freedom and Dignity*, Skinner began spelling out some of the false values that interfered with the acceptance of a scientific utopia.

One serious mistake that Western culture had made was the adoption of the fiction of the "autonomous man." Western culture was still living with the prescientific myth that human beings were free agents who were able to make their own decisions and direct their own behavior.

Two features of autonomous man are particularly troublesome. In the traditional view, a person is free. He is autonomous in the sense that his behavior is uncaused. He can therefore be held responsible for what he does and justly punished if he offends. That view, together with its associated practices, must be re-examined when a scientific analysis reveals unsuspected controlling relations between behavior and environment. Autonomous man survives in the face of all this because he [is said to be] the happy exception . . .

This escape route is slowly closed as new evidences of the predictability of human behavior are discovered. Personal exemption from a complete determinism is revoked as a scientific analysis progresses, particularly in accounting for the behavior of the individual. . . A scientific analysis naturally moves in the direction of clarifying all kinds of controlling relations.

By questioning the control exercised by

autonomous man and demonstrating the control exercised by the environment, a science of behavior also
seems to question dignity or worth. A person is responsible for his behavior, not only in the sense that he may
be justly blamed or punished when he behaves badly,
but also in the sense that he is to be given credit and
admired for his achievements. A scientific analysis shifts
the credit as well as the blame to the environment, and
traditional practices can then no longer be justified.
These are sweeping changes, and those who are committed to traditional theories and practices naturally
resist them.[6]

So much for freedom and dignity. For Skinner, that which lies
"beyond freedom and dignity," of course, is most obvious:
the systematic and organized control of human behavior
through the careful application of scientific principles.

Needless to say, *Beyond Freedom and Dignity* caused
a furor, and most critics were very upset with Skinner's
proposition that freedom and dignity were mere anachro-
nistic values impeding the march of progress. Some critics
felt that Skinner's heavy emphasis on scientism and his
chronic disaffection with traditional human values were merely
a means of twitting the public's understanding of itself. Walter
Arnold, in *Saturday Review*, queried, "What is to be thought
of all this? Is *Beyond Freedom and Dignity* perhaps a Swiftian
'modest proposal,' a deliberate deadpan put-on contrived as
a stimulus to evoke a highly aversive response?"[7] Arnold
obviously entertained the suspicion that Skinner was teasing
the public in the manner of a Diogenes, a Lenny Bruce, or a
Jerry Rubin. Peter Caws, writing in *The New Republic*,
voiced a similar concern:

The trouble with Professor Skinner's book, as with
behaviorist literature in general, is that it seems to be
designed to raise people's hackles. Consider its main
thrust—an attack on the concepts of human freedom
and human dignity and on the literature that embodies
them. Professor Skinner must know that even if these

concepts are inappropriate they are not neutral but arouse passions, especially in people who think their government and way of life are designed to protect such values; he must know that an attack on them will produce what he calls "aversive reactions"; he must know that books which produce aversive reactions are less effective in changing behavior than books which don't. Yet he marches into the temple of Western humanism and lays about him, in the grand tradition of antimetaphysical positivism.[8]

Arnold and Caws thus saw Skinner's book in the perspective of that deviant form of behavior that we have identified as oddball.

The critics clearly reaped considerable pleasure from responding to Skinner's thesis. Arnold, for example, opined, "Having said this much for the book, I must add that its most important service is the negative one of providing an example of the absurdity to which the superstition of scientism leads."[9] George Kateb, writing in *Atlantic Monthly*, saw in Skinner's work "one of the most serious threats conceivable to human survival." He concludes:

Phantasies to one side, the message is clear. Skinner believes that we can survive only if we allow a gigantic simplification of life. By that he means—he must finally mean—the atrophy of consciousness. He does not think that introspective, complex, self-doubting, self-torturing, self-indulgent, dissident, wordy people are *efficient*. He can set things up, he is sure, so that fewer such people occur. Does he not see that only silly geese lay golden eggs?[10]

The irony of Kateb's observation, of course, reduces the magnificent oddballlitry of B. F. Skinner to a position that would render future oddballs impossible.

Within the academic community of psychologist-scientist peers, *Beyond Freedom and Dignity* met with a mixed reception, but Skinner had long been in the habit of inspiring complex reactions among his peers. Willard F. Day, writing in *Contemporary Psychology,* the official review organ for the science and profession of psychology, probably came closest to the real heart of the matter: "The fact of the matter is, however, that the analogous patterns of inherent rationality that underlie Skinner's thought are radically different from those almost universally shared among members of the academic community at the present time."[11] Day goes on to recommend that a concerted effort should be made to have the underlying intellectual predispositions of Skinner's thought rendered as verbally explicit as possible so that analytic philosophers might have ample opportunity to study the ways in which Skinner's mind works! Again, the irony emerges: Skinner, the man who denies mind and asserts only behavior, is recommended for a study of his mind. In any event, like most academicians, it takes Willard Day a lot of two-dollar words to make the simple observation that he, too, believes that Skinner is an oddball.

Oscar Hobart Mowrer, himself a reformed behaviorist who saw the light and came over to the "other side," was not especially enthusiastic about Skinner's latest venture into nonhumanism. Addressing himself to the basic issue of control, Mowrer asks:

> Control *by whom*? Presumably by behavioral scientists. And suppose the scientists differ among themselves on what is good for the masses? A recent issue of the *Atlantic Monthly* carried a feature story on Skinner in which the author quotes him as having written (in one of his innumerable "daybooks" or diaries): "It may well be all up to me." It has been said that "one goes mad if one goes too far alone."[12]

Mowrer also underlines the type of concern that is generated even in sophisticates when they are confronted by the implications of a far-out theory. This issue of the control of human behavior touches individuals with a sufficient degree of alarm that the specter of dictatorship by a madman constantly looms. From Mowrer's perspective, Skinner has undoubtedly "gone too far alone."

The most comprehensive response to the scientism and operant behaviorism presented in *Beyond Freedom* has been that of Finley Carpenter, a University of Michigan professor of educational psychology. Instead of just reviewing *Beyond Freedom*, Carpenter has written a whole book about it, a work which bears the catchy title *The Skinner Primer*.[13] Carpenter's book is a balanced and unemotional account of Skinner's approach to life and morals. It systematically investigates the strengths and weaknesses of Skinnerian behaviorism and likewise telegraphs the creeping likelihood that Skinner will one day be integrated into the mainstream of conventional psychology.

Irrespective of the eventual outcome of Skinnerian theory, however, B. F. Skinner remains a highly unique personality whose life contains many lessons for the study of the social maverick. One of the most striking aspects of Skinner's behavior in this regard has been his willingness to apply his scientific belief system to the conduct of his own life, a fact which has also raised considerable public controversy. Scientism for Skinner is as much a way of life as it is a laboratory enterprise. Some years ago when he was appearing for the first time on a TV talk show, for example, Skinner had occasion to raise Montaigne's old dilemma: "If you had to choose, would you burn your children or your books?" Skinner acknowledged that he would rather burn his children because he felt that the contribution to mankind through his books was much greater than any contribution he could make through his genes. Such controversial observations tend to be greeted with public indignation but also evidence his total dedication to a thorough-going scientism. Most people could easily agree that they would rather not have Skinner as a father.

Leaving the realm of such hypothetical dilemmas, it should be pointed out that Skinner has never been loathe to practice "good science" on his own children. When his daughter Deborah was born in 1944, Skinner took a long hard look at conventional practices of infant care. He did not like what he saw, feeling that most babies were trussed up with layer after layer of diapers, bunting, nightclothes, sheets, blankets, etc. It was his judgment that so many layers of cotton could only restrict movement (operant, spontaneous behavior?) and cause rashes. Skinner proceeded to invent a controlled environment for newborn children, a fully enclosed crib that carefully controlled for temperature and humidity, thus allowing an infant to remain completely naked. His daughter Deborah spent the first two and one-half years of her life in a carefully designed "baby box." When Skinner wrote an article on his invention for a 1945 issue of *Ladies Home Journal*, many people were horrified at his proposed innovation in child-rearing practices. As Skinner's reputation for controversy continued growing, some of his critics apparently spread the rumor that his daughter had suffered severe psychological problems in her young adulthood because of her early life in the baby box. A recent cover story in *Time*, however, assured the public that Deborah has grown to full womanhood without adverse consequences.[14] Deborah herself seemed quite pleased to have B. F. Skinner as a father.

In the original 1945 article, aptly entitled "Baby in a Box," Skinner noted that his daughter had genuinely thrived in the controlled environment, seldom crying and usually demonstrating exceptional good cheer. He refuted the suggestion that such a baby box would starve the child of needed affection:

> The compartment does not ostracize the baby. The large window is no more of a social barrier than the bars of a crib. The baby follows what is going on in the room, smiles at passers-by, plays "peek-a-boo" games, and obviously delights in company. And she is handled, talked to, and played with whenever she is changed or fed, and each afternoon during a play period which is becoming longer as she grows older.
>
> The fact is that a baby will probably get more love

and affection when it is easily cared for, because the mother is not so likely to feel overworked and resentful of the demands made upon her. She will express her love in a practical way and give the baby genuinely affectionate care.

It is common practice to advise the troubled mother to be patient and tender and to enjoy her baby. And, of course, this is what the baby needs. But it is the exceptional mother who can fill this prescription upon demand, especially if there are other children in the family and she has no help. We need to go one step further and treat the mother with affection also. Simplified child care will give mother love a chance.[15]

A careful reading of Skinner's work amply demonstrates, I think, that he is not some sort of mad scientific ogre who is out to rule the world but rather a dedicated scientist who invests his energies in providing practical solutions to a large variety of human problems. Even in this sensitive and sensible article about infant care, however, Skinner concludes: "There is a plausible connection between health and happiness and the surroundings we have provided, and I am quite sure that our success is not an accident. The experiment should, of course, be repeated again and again with different babies and different parents."[16] To the last, he remains a scientist committed to "the experiment" as the means of advancing human progress. It is, perhaps, this strange admixture of cold science and warm concern about people's problems that has so confused and infuriated Skinner's critics.

This remarkable capacity to infuriate is unquestionably one of Skinner's most salient characteristics. In many ways, he seems to be a man with a long, invisible pin walking about looking for cherished bubbles that he might burst. In the pursuit of his own unique understanding of science, for example, Skinner has taken considerable pains to point out that many current brands of science are somewhat less than meaningful. He especially delights in taking pot shots at the classical hypothetico-deductive method which he seems to regard as the last refuge of the impoverished mind. The hypothetico-deductive method, of course, is usually considered to be the real bread and butter of the science business. In this model, the scientist carefully observes an area of scientific investigation, gathers together a series of ideas about the relations that exist between various events in the field of observation, develops a theory that will explain the relationships between the important factors or variables, deduces a hypothesis that will test the supposed relationships, performs a series of experiments that rigorously quantify the variables in question, and then proceeds to publish the results of the experiment so that professional colleagues can marvel at his ingenuity and creative research. Skinner thinks that this is a lot of nonsense. He feels that this is just another aspect of mythology, in this case the myth of Man Thinking, a myth that he holds right on par with Autonomous Man. In his own words:

> It is a mistake to identify scientific practice with the formalized constructions of statistics and scientific method. These disciplines have their place, but it does not coincide with the place of scientific research. They offer *a* method of science, but not, as is so often implied, *the* method.[17]

In a well-known article entitled "A Case History in Scientific Method," Skinner hilariously described his own scientific behavior involved in the "discovery" of operant conditioning. His description is consistent with his own theory of environmental control in pointing out how he was time and time again compelled to follow the lines of investigation laid down by accidental events within the laboratory. Skinner sums up his scientific behavior in this regard in a series of principles that might prove helpful to the fledgling scientist: (1) "When you run into something interesting, drop everything else and study it"; (2) "Some ways of doing research are easier than others"; (3) "Some people are lucky"; and (4) "Apparatuses sometimes break down." Skinner concludes:

> The notes, data, and publications which I have

examined do not show that I ever behaved in the manner of Man Thinking as described by John Stuart Mill or John Dewey or in reconstructions of scientific behavior by philosophers of science. I never faced a Problem which was more than the eternal problem of finding order. I never attacked a problem by constructing a Hypothesis. I never deduced Theorems or submitted them to Experimental Check. So far as I can see, I had no preconceived Model of behavior—certainly not a physiological or a mentalistic one and, I believe, not a conceptual one.[18]

The brand of science advocated by B. F. Skinner, consistent with his arguments in *Beyond Freedom and Dignity*, resists the plausibility of assigning credit or blame even to the scientist himself. True to his view, Skinner maintains that scientific behavior is itself controlled by various environmental contingencies, which heavily influence the activities of the scientist. With undeniable consistency, Skinner analyzes his own behavior in his own laboratory according to the same principles of operant conditioning that he believes to be functional in the control of rats and pigeons in his Skinner box. It is essentially because of this highly consistent view of behavioral events that Skinner was able to make the leap to an entire society functioning according to principles of operant conditioning. For Skinner, there is precious little difference between *Walden Two*, the behavior of rats and pigeons in the Skinner box, or the behavior of the world's leading scientists. Many scientists remain unflattered by the comparison.

Perhaps the most striking aspect of Skinnerian science is its thorough-going emphasis on discovering solutions to problems. In this respect, Skinnerian behaviorism is almost exclusively an applied science, the strongest feature of which is its power to provide methods for the definition and resolution of a whole host of problems. Skinner is a complete pragmatist who embraces the belief that "if it works, it's good." Indeed, one of the things that seem most annoying to Skinner's scientific peers is his unique capacity to make things work and to provide simple solutions for seemingly complex problems. Skinner is the consummate problem-solver. Although many of his proferred solutions to mankind's problems have been rejected by others, such proposed solutions have seldom been rejected on the basis of their workability. People object to his values and to what they might consider to be an incomplete or defective view of human functioning. But it is difficult to point a finger at Skinner and chastise him with the proclamation "It won't work."

Of the hundreds of projects that Skinner has undertaken as an active problem-solver, there is only one that he failed to bring to satisfactory completion. Skinner published a history of this project in a paper entitled "Pigeons in a Pelican." This project was conducted during World War II under the auspices of the Naval Research Laboratory and was called ORCON, derived from the words "organic control." In the confines of his laboratory, Skinner had long been investigating methods of producing behavioral control of animals and had achieved some remarkable results, especially with pigeons. In Skinner's laboratory, pigeons had been taught to dance (a simple two-step and fox-trot rather than the more complex boogie-woogies that were just coming into vogue), to play ping-pong (not necessarily of competitive calibre, mind you), as well as a host of behaviors that pigeons did not typically pursue. At the time, the United States military was testing an air-to-ground missile called the "Pelican," and military science was searching for a homing device that would guide the missile directly to a target. Skinner conceived the idea of fitting a pigeon in the nose of the Pelican and using the homing abilities of the pigeon as the basic guidance system. He had begun some preliminary research on this project and had discovered a practical and economic method of training pigeons to perform the task flawlessly. He was then asked to present a demonstration with his colleagues of the project to a committee of the country's top scientists for application to the war effort. The demonstration was arranged and Skinner's pigeons performed flawlessly. "But the spectacle of a living pigeon carrying out its assignment, no matter how beautifully, simply reminded the committee of how utterly fantastic our proposal was."[19] The "Pigeon in a Pelican" project was not encouraged with military funding, and Skinner was forced to scrap the project despite its proven practicality. Skinner recognized that he had a crackpot idea, and yet he continued to defend the importance of the crackpot idea for human progress:

> If I were to conclude that crackpot ideas were to be encouraged, I should probably be told that psychology has already had more than its share of them. If it has, they have been entertained by the wrong people. Reacting against the excesses of psychological quackery, psychologists have developed an enormous concern for scientific respectability. They constantly warn their students against questionable facts and unsupported theories. As a result, the usual Ph.D. thesis is a model of compulsive cautiousness, advancing only the most timid conclusions thoroughly hedged about with qualifications. But it is just the man capable of such admirable caution who needs a touch of uncontrolled speculation. Possibly a generous exposure to psychological science fiction would help. Project pigeon might be said to support that view. Except with respect to its avowed goal, it was, as I see it, highly productive; and this was in large measure because my colleagues and I knew that, in the eyes of the world, we were crazy.[20]

B. F. Skinner is well aware that the world regards him as crazy, but he has been consistently willing to risk the social stigma involved in being labeled an oddball. Oddballs are not motivated by social approval, and it is precisely because of this fact that they are able to make their highly unique contributions. Skinner's accomplishments are legion, and the dividends are reaped by his accomplishments almost daily. Behavioral techniques continue to display a capacity to be adapted to almost any environment, including the classroom, the hospital, industry, mental health settings, homes for the aged, and so forth. Behavior modification has become an accepted technique for ameliorating a host of human problems ranging from toilet-training retarded children to the reformation of prison systems. There is no doubt in my mind that future generations will canonize B. F. Skinner as a scientific saint. In the view of current humanity, however, Skinner is an oddball. By his own admission, he is an oddball.

In a particularly ringing passage of *Walden Two*, Frazier attacks Burris with the basic problem of being an oddball:

> You think I'm conceited, aggressive, tactless, selfish. You're convinced that I'm completely insensitive to my effect on others, except when the effect is calculated. You can't see in me any personal warmth. You're sure that I'm one who couldn't possibly be a genuine member of any community . . . . Shall we say that as a person I'm a complete failure and have done with it?

There are painful and difficult issues involved for anyone who risks the prospect of being different. Skinner has taken the risks and has suffered the consequences. As he himself maintains, however, "Behavior is a function of its consequences." Perhaps oddball behavior is produced and controlled by subtle rewards evoked from the environment. From the standpoint of B. F. Skinner, the anti-autonomous man, oddballs themselves are merely products of their environment, which is to say that oddballs are made and not born. In the last analysis, Skinner steals the thunder from oddballitry itself.

14
Toward a Theory of Individuality

FROM ERICH VON Daniken to B. F. Skinner, from oddball ideas to oddball behavior, from oddball artistry to oddball scientism, even from ancient societies to future utopias—throughout these discussions and investigations of highly unique and diverse personalities, the underlying concern has been the theme of what it means to be an individual. The approach taken here has maintained that individuality is a desirable good and that the best examples of individuality are to be found in certain oddball characters who demonstrate the capacity to distinguish themselves from their social surroundings and contextual milieu. It should be quite clear that this study has taken a highly prejudicial view: in terms of the respective merits of communitarian versus individualistic values, I have consistently opted to emphasize individual considerations. I trust that the bias has been quite undisguised. In most philosophies of individualism, there is a quite explicit assumption that the welfare of the society will itself flourish only if the individual is free to pursue his own desires. Whether or not this is true is quite another question, but on a less grandiose scale I believe that oddballs are good for society; social traditions can maintain their vigor only when subjected to the kind of questioning that is provided by the social maverick. In this sense, I am as much in favor of traditions and conventions as I am in admiration of those individuals who challenge the conventions. (Livable societies are as much characterized by the order generated by social conventions as by the chaos that follows in the wake of the deviant.)

In this final chapter, I will attempt to synthesize some of the themes that have occurred somewhat lambently in the consideration of the oddball. It is time to move on more directly to a consideration of what it means to be a person capable of functioning in a highly individualized fashion. Individuality is a slippery concept and, as we have seen, can be manifested in manifold ways. If we are to evolve a philosophic attitude toward individuality, it is probably best to begin with the basics, including a simple definition of terms.

The word *individual* derives from the Latin *individuus*, which can be quite directly translated as "indivisible." In this sense, any object in the animate or inanimate world that exists independently and in its own right can be said to be an individual. A rock is an individual, a tree is an individual, a cat is an individual, John Doe is an individual. The wind is not an individual, a bag of jelly beans is not an individual, the United States of America is not an individual. In this metaphysical sense, anything that has a separate and distinct existence in the real world can legitimately be termed an individual. The discussion that has been pursued in this volume obviously includes this fundamental notion of individuality but is likewise much more specific. We are here examining individuality from the viewpoint of human personality and those special characteristics that distinguish one person from another person or group of persons. In this sense, individuality refers to "that which sets one apart from others." Whereas the individual is a given of existence, individuality is an achievement of life processes. It is not given. It is arrived at by conflict and personal struggle.

In my opinion, this phenomenon is better described as "individuality" than "individualism." Individualism is a frankly political doctrine inspired by John Locke, John Stuart Mill, Herbert Spencer, and thinkers of similar ilk. As a political view, individualism maintains that individual persons are the ultimate political units, both logically and morally, prior to the social group or state; thus, individuals are understood to be the ends for which the state is merely the means. It should be pointed out that a psychology of individuality need not be tied to a political philosophy of individualism. Alexander Solzhenitsyn, for example, the highly individualized Russian novelist, neither espouses nor desires to live under a political philosophy of individualism. It is probably fair to say that a democratic political system is likely to be more supportive of individuality than is a socialist system, but it is also fair to say that highly individualized persons are likely to emerge from different political systems. In the main, authentic individuality is probably independent of political process.

Individuality is best understood, then, as a psychosocial phenomenon involving a complex set of interactions between the normalizing influence of the social group and the innate or acquired drive to be oneself. If individuality has any valid psychological meaning, it must be understood as a characteristic or constellation of characteristics that sets a person apart. Apart from what? The social group, of course. The interconnections between the individual and the social group are so consuming that it is difficult to understand one without the other. There can be no social group that is not in itself an aggregate of individuals (in the sense of objects that exist in their own right) nor can there be an individual (in the sense of something that sets one apart) without a social group as a reference point.

We may well be treading a thin line between philosophic intrigue and semantic madness, but these are important considerations. Some individuals are necessary for the constitution and maintenance of the social group and other individuals are necessary for the evolution and alteration of the social group. Highly individualized persons who depart from the normal standards of group thinking and group behavior act as "scouts" by which more conventional individuals are able to test out and plot the possible directions of social evolution and human advance. When Darwin set forth the highly unique conception of human evolutionary descent from other animal forms, he gave mankind an opportunity to redefine basic ways in which it had come to understand itself as well as an opportunity to take cognizance of future directions. The person who achieves a high degree of individuality thus serves to open up different pathways and then the social group can reconsider its destiny.

When an individual becomes sufficiently oddball, therefore, he performs a valuable function for the social group in the sense that he explores the outer limits and/or unexplored areas of human experience. It is the oddball who is the source of cultural advance. David Miller, in his excellent book on individualism, has gone to great pains to consolidate a similar argument. Miller states:

> The purpose of this book is to explain the meaning of individualism and to defend the belief that every worthy and significant change that is planned and deliberately undertaken in a society has its origin in the mind of an individual. The individual—not the community, not public opinion, not external environmental forces—is the source of new ideas that enable society to make changes for the achievement of ideals that in the short run at least are fairly explicitly stated, and in the long run are consistent with the higher hopes of the members of society.[1]

Miller, however, takes a benign view of the highly individualized person and never ventures into notions of oddballitry. In the main, he wants his individuals to be socially acceptable:

> Individualism as we understand it always involves novelty, the creativity of an enterprising person who is instrumental in effecting new and, purportedly, more effective ways of achieving socially acceptable goals by using means in accord with our traditional values. The individual is an innovator whose new proposal is directed to his community, small or large.[2]

Most of the oddballs in this study have achieved or are in the process of achieving creative cultural changes, but I do not think that their individual goals have been "socially acceptable" or "in accord with traditional values." Miller's proposal tends to emasculate authentic individuality by removing from it any abrasive or threatening quality. B. F. Skinner, for example, is an amazingly innovative thinker, and yet he has mounted a direct and persistent attack on such traditional values as freedom and dignity. Highly innovative people generally tend to wreak havoc on "socially acceptable goals" and "traditional values." In most instances, the highly individualized person is a thorn in the side of the social group for the very reason that he is different and not "in accord." In the same manner, the social response to the "different" individual typically accentuates the nature of the difference so that counterattacks and consternation provide an even clearer frame of reference by which the innovator becomes increasingly individualized. As Kenneth Tynan observed with regard to Lenny Bruce, "Constant abrasive irritation produces the pearl: it is the disease of the oyster." The oddball is the pearl of the social group; but the oddball is made possible only through the abrasive irritation that is the clash between values.

In short, the transactions that occur between conserving individuals and innovating individuals are usually not of an orderly and peaceful nature. It is not the function of the oddball to align himself with acceptable values, and, in this sense, it is not possible to be both highly individualized and highly socialized. One cannot be both a conserver and an innovator. To be individualized is precisely to be set apart and to be at odds with the social conventions, at least in that area of social commerce in which one has achieved a high degree of individualization. Igor Stravinsky, for example, was never in contest with most aspects of cultural tradition. And yet, when it came to music and art, Stravinsky was highly anticonventional. He was not merely unconventional; he was anticonventional. Stravinsky's music upset people for the very reason that he overturned the accepted apple cart of musical conventions. Oddballs do not adjust to the social conventions, and the conservers of the social conventions resist adjustment to the oddball. The interactions that take place between conserving individuals and innovating individuals are, therefore, fraught with conflict, and the dynamics of individuality always involve conflictual interplay between the oddball and the social group.

Within the oddball himself, however, there is typically little conflict between his own emerging values and the so-called internalized values of the social group. The oddball may be at war with convention, but this warring with convention is directed outside of himself. It is my belief that authentic individuality involves the ability to resolve possible intra-psychic conflicts between "doing the accepted thing" and "doing one's own thing." The conflict between personal and social values does not take place within the oddball but rather between the oddball and the social group. The conflict, so to speak, goes public because the oddball opts for his own unique behavior or idea in a clearly decisive fashion. The essential dynamic of individualization rests primarily in the oddball's ability to dismiss possible internal conflicts between his own values and the perceived values of the social group. In *Walden Two*, for example, Skinner's alter egos, Burris and Frazier, demonstrate the internal conflict between the warring factions within Skinner himself. Skinner wants to evolve his own vision, and yet he is aware of the clash between his vision and the conventional system. But Skinner resolves the conflict inside himself; he dismisses the conventional view and chooses to be purely Skinnerian. Thus, the oddball is able to use the conventions of the social group as a frame of reference against which individuality is tested and refined.

Thus, it would seem that the dynamic interplay between the oddball and the social group is composed of the following elements:

(1) Individuals come together to share and conserve a cultural frame of reference or set of social values and conventions. Many aspects of this frame of reference are implicit and unarticulated.

(2) An individual rejects some aspect of the accepted frame of reference in preference for some innovative behavior or idea. Implicit aspects of the cultural frame of reference are brought more clearly into focus, and explicit aspects of the conventional value system are directly challenged.

(3) Public conflict takes place between the social group that seeks to conserve the traditional values and the deviant individual.

(4) The reaction of conserving individuals is to reaffirm and refine the traditional values and conventional wisdom.

(5) The reaction of the oddball is to pursue further and with increased vigor the unique nature of the innovative idea or behavior.

(6) A latency period takes place in which the oddball innovation begins to acquire social support. This newly acquired social support system tends to modify or make acceptable some of the outlandish aspects of the oddball's individuality.

(7) The distinction between the traditional value and the innovation becomes somewhat blurred.

(8) The cultural frame of reference gradually adjusts to the extent that the less outlandish aspects of the oddball idea or behavior are integrated into the conventional mainstream.

(9) With the passing of generations, the oddball is canonized as a father of cultural traditions.

Although this brief description conveniently ignores some of the more complex aspects of social interaction and sociocultural history, it does account for the way in which society attempts to deal with the brilliant deviant. Darwin, Moses, Ezekiel, Diogenes, and Freud, as well as many oddballs not studied in this volume, have long been integrated into the mainstream, and their contributions have become a part of our cultural heritage. Bruce, Rubin, von Daniken, Skinner, Stravinsky, and Joyce are so recent that their respective transmogrifications have not been completed. Perhaps some of them—like the Fowlers—will be assigned a footnote in the history of oddballs and social institutions. For reasons that are not altogether clear to me, some oddballs are passed over despite the fact that they scale the heights of individuality. Obviously, some apparently brilliant deviations turn out to be little more than blind alleys for the great majority of conserving individuals and, for this reason, fail to influence the cultural mainstream. If it were not for the wasted antics of recognized failures, however, most social groups would merely carry out accepted tasks in a highly routinized fashion. Only a small percentage of genuine oddballs ever become cultural heroes, but weirdoes everywhere are important in keeping the cultural dialectic alive and well.

Which brings us conveniently to the next point. Even if it is granted that oddballs, in the long run, are good for social progress, what good are they to you and me, here and now, and in the short run? Why bother with this whole business of individuality, oddballitry, and what it means to be an individual?

How we define ourselves makes a difference. All too often many of us take the easy path and define ourselves in terms of current social conventions. For example, I am a father to these children, a husband to this wife, a title in the institution, an officer in this organization, a member of this political party, a dweller in this city, an owner of this car, a thinker of this school of thought, a smoker of this brand of cigarette, a consumer of this product, a practitioner of this kind of behavior. Labels, labels everywhere, and who the hell am I? What makes me distinct and unique and different from everybody else who shares the same labels?

As social groups grow more complex and institutionalized, the role of the individual *qua* individual becomes progressively obscure. Persons become interchangeable. This is especially true in the occupational marketplace where people are trained to abolish idiosyncrasies so that they can more easily be plugged in to each other's slots. I will not review the litany of horrors that is currently alleged to be part of contemporary human existence, but it is probably safe to say that life in urbania is almost as depersonalizing as everyone says it is. Many of us are so involved in acquiring the skills and attitudes that seem necessary for survival in a complex society that we have little opportunity to develop ourselves, especially those aspects that are not encouraged by social or institutional pressure.

The social and psychological literature of the twentieth century bears avid testimony to the cloudy consciousness of contemporary man, and a whole new set of personal-social constructs has come into vogue: *angst, authenticity, depersonalization, identity, existential self, mass society, social repression, alienation, new morality,* etc. The gist of most current literature is that social conditions stink, and if one is to be authentically oneself, one must attack and modify existing social conditions. Students feel that school systems are atrocious, so they attack the administrators of the schools and universities. Blacks assail the systematic prejudice that has created the urban ghetto and the hopelessness of the welfare system. Feminists attack language as the creation of a male chauvinist system, and we are stuck with the oddities of *chairpersons, weatherpersons, firepersons, policepersons, mailpersons,* and even *malepersons.* It is well and good to address one's energies to the repair and renovation of defective social conditions but not at the expense of the individual and the very processes of individualization. Movements are instruments of the social

group; with the exception of the founding oddball, movements do not provide a vehicle by which individuals achieve a
sense of uniqueness and individuality.

With the increasing awareness of the many ways in
which individual behavior is culturally determined—insights,
by the way, that have come primarily from Freud and
Skinner—there has been a tendency to view the personal ego
as a social institution. "Movement" philosophies—including
feminism, civil rights, student activism, and New Left liber-
alism—actively abet the notion that one cannot become fully
oneself without joining the relevant movement and correcting
the relevant inadequacies of the relevant social institution.
Politics and personality become confused, and the individual
is easily translated into a vehicle for social change. Carol
Hanisch, an ardent spokeswoman for woman's rights, has
recently published an article, for example, defending the proposition that "the personal is political."[3] I disagree. The interactions between the individual and the social system are
complex and consuming, but they are not merely different
sides of the same coin. The individual in search of his or her
own individuality often brings about striking changes in the
social group in which he or she abides. Such changes,
however, are a consequence rather than the sole purpose of
individualization. Individuals do not exist solely for the purpose of conserving or changing social conditions, and the
individual is not a social institution. It is a mistake to identify
personal fulfillment with political activism.

Marshall Berman, in his excellent study of political
theory entitled *The Politics of Authenticity*, makes the following observation:

> The search for authenticity, nearly everywhere we find it
> in modern times, is bound up with a radical rejection of
> things as they are. It begins with an insistence that the
> social and political structures men live in are keeping the
> self stifled, chained down, locked up. It argues that only

if the old structure is renovated, or if a new one is built from the ground up—or if the old one is wrecked and nothing put in its place, so that men may live without any structure at all—only then can the self come into its own. It asks what is to be done and tries to do it. Thus the desire for authenticity has emerged in modern society as one of the most politically explosive of human impulses.[4]

When social institutions are the primary concern—whether that concern is manifested as a conservation or alteration of the social institution—the individual gets lost. Without the perspective that individuality is a desirable end in itself, even those who espouse a political philosophy of radical individualism find themselves locked in the contradictions of thinking in anti-individualistic terms. A genuine philosophy of individuality must maintain that the individual is not *for* the social institution in any sense, neither *for* the purpose of conserving the social institution nor *for* the purpose of radically altering the social institution. Many things that individuals do for their own purposes and in pursuit of their own individuality drastically affect the climate of the social group. The individual uses the social group as a frame of reference by which his or her own individuality may be pursued, but a theory of individuality would be defective if it overemphasized the social consequences of individuality to the detriment of the individual *qua* individual.

It is in the oddball that the real lessons of individuality are to be learned. Many reference points exist from which the phenomenon of individualization can be viewed, just as a variety of philosophical, psychological, and sociological constructs have been advanced to label and define this phenomenon. Authenticity, self-realization, creative selfhood, self-actualization, ego-identity, existential selfhood—all of these are attempts to crystallize aspects of human behavior that cannot be explained by reference to a set of cultural guidelines. In my own review of highly individualized persons, I have been struck by certain characteristics of the individualizing self that seem to recur. I offer the following notions not as a set of common dimensions so much as likely dynamisms that tend to be operative in processes of individualization.

1) Oddballs tend to be moved by *a sense of personal agency*, and they usually regard themselves as having some special mission. (In the psychiatric literature this condition is usually diagnosed as "paranoia" manifested in illusions of grandeur.) This sense of personal agency may be prompted by a variety of inner needs, including the need for achievement through the accomplishment of something difficult, the need to exhibit oneself and be on display, the need to overcome opposition in a direct and forceful fashion, the need to be understood and to have a special place, and so on. The inner need may even be prompted by some dynamic of counteraction or overcompensation. Napoleon, for example, is said to have been interested in conquering the world primarily because he felt ashamed of his extremely short stature! The more diagnostically inclined will see in oddballs some manifestation of psychiatric dynamics; I prefer simply to recognize a sense of personal agency prompted by a variety of inner needs. Individualization is associated with some form of magnificent obsession.

2) The oddball's sense of personal agency is explicitly characterized by *a belief in self rather than a belief in others*. (Again, in the psychiatric literature, this condition is usually referred to as "primary narcissism" and typically carries a pejorative connotation.) This deep conviction and involvement in one's own point of view often manifests itself as irreverence for the opinions of others and disrespect for local customs. In the oddball, iconoclasm toward accepted traditions and commonly held views is typically a function of the individual's pursuit of a unique vision rather than a pointless attack on the establishment. The oddball has an alternate belief system, not merely a chaotic urge to destroy authority.

Jerry Rubin, for all his social anarchism, was able to present and defend a platform of self-expression.

3) Oddballs are further distinguished by *a sense of persistence and dedication that functions independently of the consequences.* (In the psychiatric jargon, the specter of the "psychopathic personality" begins to loom.) Oddballs continue to do their own thing irrespective of social implications and personal consequences. They tend to be fearless toward authority and independent of public opinion. They are not merely self-starters. They are also self-sustainers and are able to pursue their own vision no matter what people think. They may sometimes enjoy public consternation, but they are seldom defeated by social antagonism. Freud's remark, "many enemies, much honor," is an indication that oddballs can find self-approval even in situations that are threatening to most people. Individualized persons maintain dignity and self-esteem even in the presence of adverse social pressure; oddballs are not especially taken with the task of pleasing people and do not make a religious creed of social amenity.

4) Oddballs evince *a special interest in the unexplained, the unknown, and the unnoticed.* (Psychiatrically, the passive-aggressive personality is also known to have a tendency to uncover irksome details.) Erich von Daniken, for example, has made a career exploring those archaeological details that do not fit with accepted theories, and Stravinsky was constantly concerned with discovering discordant intervals in the conventional musical scales. This passion for the unknown or the undiscovered can be motivated equally by disenchantment with the accepted system and the desire to pursue a novel interpretation. Creative innovations by oddballs are often a function of an inability to overlook discrepant data. Darwin, for example, felt compelled to explain the biological evidence that conflicted with creationist theology. Oddballs are drawn to discrepant data like turtles to the sea. The creativity that is associated with the innovative person involves a capacity to be captured by

the unexplicable and a desire to make sense of things that more conventional persons simply tend to overlook or to dismiss. Individualization seems to require an attraction to the novel and unusual combined with a disinclination to take things for granted. Novelty is a periodic need in the process of individualization.

5) Oddballs are comfortable with a *unique experience of reality*, and they may even take pleasure in inflicting this separate sense of reality on others. (From the psychiatric perspective, this is a characteristic that is associated with "schizophrenia" and is an indication of serious disturbance.) It is commonplace for oddballs to view the world in strikingly different terms than is typical for other members of the social group. Indeed, a good definition of the social maverick is someone whose inner experience of reality differs significantly from the experience of reality that is held in common by members of the society. This awareness of disparity by the oddball is savored and heightened rather than discarded in favor of adaptation to the common sense of reality. The oddball attempts to publicize his unique view and to convert others to an alternate reality. When Moses, for example, was working out his experience of a "One God," he did not hide in the mountains at the foot of the burning bush; rather he attempted to convert the Hebrews to religious monotheism. The highly individualized do not believe in absolute realities that are not of their own making, and they actively seek the responsibility of developing their own realities. The oddball is a kind of "reality thief," who nudges others to question accepted realities. In this way, however, unique individuals are also capable of expanding the reality experience that is shared by the social group.

6) Oddballs are *not especially private but seek the public forum*. (Both the "manic personality" as well as the "exhibitionist" provide much grist for the psychiatric mill.) Social mavericks are not embarrassed by what they think and do, and they are disinclined toward "hiding their lights

under a bushel," as the Bible has it. Ezekiel and Diogenes, for example, were not even loath to place their genitals on parade so as to make a point about their individual perspectives. Highly individualized persons feel no shame in being an individual and are always willing to wax eloquent or otherwise in public. Nor do they keep their disagreements with society to themselves but are willing to risk or even provoke external conflict in the service of their own individuality. The highly individualized person may well be sensitive to the tensions between his own need for self-exploration and the conventions of the social group, but he is not deterred by the prospect of public conflict. He may even seek to cleanse the culture from the demons of counterfeit conventions.

Most of us are probably unable to achieve the degree of individualization that is characteristic of the oddballs examined in this study, but we are able to be ourselves in our own ways. I doubt, however, that it is possible for one to be a complete individual without some sense of personal agency, without some belief in oneself, without some willingness to accept the consequences of being unique, without some passion for the unknown or undefined, without some sense of a unique reality, and without some occasion to defend publicly—even in a small group—that which one holds sacred. In an exaggerated fashion, the social maverick lays bare the basic issues about what it means to be an individual and points out the various paths by which individualization can be found. The paths of the genuine oddballs are perhaps more crooked than yours or mine need to be. Nonetheless, "Improvement makes straight roads; but the crooked roads without Improvement are roads of Genius."[5] Real oddballs demonstrate genius in individualization and act as examples for us all.

With individuality, as with any area of human thought and behavior, genius is a rare phenomenon. For the majority of individuals, the path to being oneself lies somewhere between a saying of Friedrich Nietzsche and a saying of

Henry David Thoreau. Nietzsche, writing in the frenzied political atmosphere of nineteenth century Germany, averred: "No shepherd and one herd! Everybody wants the same, everybody is the same: whoever feels different goes voluntarily into a madhouse." Thoreau, in the quiet solitude of Walden Pond, maintained: "If a man does not keep pace with his companions, it may be that he steps to the music of a different drummer. Let him keep pace with that which he hears, however measured or far away." The much-observed thin line between genius and insanity may be even thinner than was thought. In contemporary society, if you are odd, you may well be thought crazy. Such are the conventions of a psychiatricized society.

Are the oddballs crazy? I suppose that some are mad and some are not. Insanity, after all, is just a point of view. Whether Ezekiel was a paranoid schizophrenic, a prophet, or an oddball is simply a function of the diagnostic system that one employs. Recent trends in psychiatry, led by such psychiatric stalwarts as Thomas Szasz and R. D. Laing, have attempted to discourage the use of psychiatric nomenclature for individuals who are simply different. Laing defends the view that the "mental patients" who live at Kingsley Hall, a hospital which he administers, are as sensible in their individual ways as anybody else. He crystallizes the difference between "people on the inside" and "people on the outside" in the following fashion:

> The disagreement between the people who live in the building and those who do not is about morals. All people decide which thoughts, feelings, acts, persons and groups of persons to call right or wrong, good or bad, clean or dirty, true or false, real or unreal, sane or insane, and so on. Western society interrogates people or groups of people to learn if they assign to particular thoughts, feelings, acts, persons and groups of persons the labels which it believes they ought to. Those who live at Kingsley Hall often do not apply the labels "correctly," and know it. If people in Western society do not, do they

have a right to live outside a mental hospital? Those who live at Kingsley Hall affirm that they do. Not all who live outside the building agree.

When residents behave in ways which are considered strange, they alarm some people outside the building. A man, aged twenty-eight, who lived at Kingsley Hall would walk into neighborhood pubs and coffee shops and, without saying a word to anyone, would pick up glasses from tables or counters, drink the contents and walk out. If a door to a house was left open he would enter and sit on a chair in the drawing-room until someone of the house would see him. Then he would get up and walk out quietly. He never said anything to threaten anyone and he never touched anyone, but he unnerved people. People would approach him in the street to offer the unsolicited advice that he would "feel better" if he were in a mental hospital.[6]

Society will always have difficulty dealing with the different individual, whether that person happens to be labeled insane, prophetic, or oddball. People who do not behave in conventional ways will disturb people who do. But hospitals are for people who are in pain and distress, physical or psychological, and not for people who are simply different. And labels are threatening. There is no doubt in my mind that many of us toe the line in society primarily because we fear the risk of diagnosis. Is pyschiatry an instrument of repression, even in a supposedly free society? Is its object to train people in adjustment rather than to help individuals to realize themselves? Is psychiatry driving healthy madness out of the world? I'd rather bet on madness than psychiatry.

I will close now with one last quotation, this one from Ken Kesey, a marvelous nut in his own right. Dispensing some sage psychiatric advice, one of Kesey's characters points out the awful fact that psychiatry has reduced genuine madness to a mere diagnostic system:

He had only smiled, condescendingly and therapeutically. "No Leland, not you. You, and in fact quite a lot of your generation, have in some way been exiled from that particular sanctuary. It's become almost impossible for you to 'go mad' in the classical sense. At one time people conveniently 'went mad' and were never heard from again. Like a character in a romantic novel. But now" — And I think he even went so far as to yawn — "you are too hip to yourself on a psychological level. You all are too intimate with too many of the symptoms of insanity to be caught completely off your guard. Another thing: all of you have a talent for releasing frustration through clever fantasy. And you, you are the worst of the lot on that score. So . . . you may be neurotic as hell for the rest of your life, and miserable, maybe even do a short hitch at Bellevue and certainly good for another five years of a paying patient—but I'm afraid never completely out." He leaned back in his elegant Lounge-o-Chair. "Sorry to disappoint you but the best I can offer is plain old schizophrenia with delusional tendencies."[7]

I like my own diagnostic system better.

Chapter Notes

Chapter 2—Erich von Daniken

1. Erich von Daniken, *Gods from Outer Space*, Bantam Books, New York, c. 1968, p. viii.
2. Erich von Daniken, *Chariots of the Gods?* Bantam Books, New York, c. 1968, p. 99.
3. Ibid., p. 50.
4. Ibid., p. 30.
5. Ibid., pp. 29-30.

Suggested Reading:
C. W. Ceram, *Gods, Graves, and Scholars*, Alfred Knopf, New York, (Revised Edition) 1967.

Chapter 3—Charles Darwin

1. C. H. Waddington, "Theories of Evolution," in *A Century of Darwin*, ed. by Samuel Anthony Barnett, Books for Libraries Press, Freeport, New York, c. 1958, p. 1.
2. For an excellent account of the ongoing relationship between Darwin and Henslow, including many previously unpublished letters, see Nora Barlow, *Darwin and Henslow: The Growth of an Idea*, UCLA Press, Los Angeles, 1967.
3. Barlow, op. cit., p. xii.
4. Waddington, op. cit., p. 4.
5. Wilfrid Le Gros Clark, "The Study of Man's Descent," in Barnett, op. cit., p. 173.
6. *Forerunners of Darwin: 1745-1859*, ed. by Bentley Glass, Owsei Temkin, and William L. Strauss, Jr., Baltimore, The Johns Hopkins Press, c. 1959, from the Preface.

Chapter 4—Moses Speaks

1. For an excellent review of the Pentateuchal traditions, see Martin Noth's *A History of Pentateuchal Traditions*, trans. by Bernhard W. Anderson, Prentice-Hall, Englewood Cliffs, New Jersey, 1972.
2. Mircea Eliade, *Cosmos and History: The Myth of the Eternal Return*, Harper and Row, New York, 1954, pp. 3-5.
3. Harold H. Rowley, *From Moses to Qumran*, Books for Libraries Press, Freeport, New York, 1963, p. 48.

Chapter 5—Diogenes of Sinope

1. Diogenes Laertius, *Lives of Eminent Philosophers*, Vol. II, trans. by R. D. Hicks, Harvard University Press, Cambridge, Mass., 1925, p. 55.
2. Ibid., p. 51.
3. Ibid., p. 63.
4. Ibid., p. 35. Also recounted by Plutarch in his *Lives*.
5. Ibid., p. 49.
6. Ibid., p. 71.
7. Ibid., p. 43.
8. Ibid., p. 77.
9. Ibid., p. 49.
10. Ibid., p. 49.
11. Ibid., p. 63.
12. Ibid., p. 43.
13. Ibid., pp. 59-60.
14. Ibid., p. 57.
15. Ibid., p. 67.
16. Ibid., p. 52.
17. Ibid., p. 51.
18. Ibid., p. 81.
19. Ibid., p. 65.
20. Ibid., p. 25.
21. Ibid., p. 33.
22. Ibid., p. 75.
23. J. M. Rist, *Stoic Philosophy*, Cambridge at the University Press, 1969, pp. 58-59.

24. Theodor Gomperz, *The Greek Thinkers*, Vol. 2, London, John Murray Publishers, 1905, pp. 151-152.

Chapter 6—The Prophet Ezekiel

1. Stephen F. Winward, *A Guide to the Prophets*, John Knox Press, Richmond, Virginia, 1968, p. 21.
2. Abraham J. Heschel, *The Prophets*, Harper and Row, New York, 1962, p. 409.
3. *The Old Testament of the Holy Bible*, Confraternity Edition, Commentaries by Joseph A. Grispino, Guild Press, New York, 1965, p. 1464.
4. Winward, op. cit., p. 157.
5. Ibid., pp. 157-158.
6. Edith Hamilton, *Spokesmen for God*, Norton, New York, 1936, p. 182.
7. Ibid., pp. 185-186.

Suggested Reading:
R. B. Y. Scott, *The Relevance of the Prophets,* Macmillan, New York, 1944.
Emil G. Kraeling, *The Prophets*, Rand-McNally, New York, 1969.
Brooke Peters Church, *The Private Lives of the Prophets*, Rinehart, New York, 1953.

Chapter 7—Jerry Rubin

1. Jerry Rubin, *Do It!*, Simon and Schuster, New York, 1970, pp. 142-143.
2. Ibid., pp. 58-59.
3. Ibid., p. 203.
4. Ibid., p. 208.
5. Note: I had intended to review Hoffman's classic masterpiece *Steal This Book!*, but it had been stolen from all the public libraries in the City of Chicago.
6. Jerry Rubin, op. cit., pp. 83-84.

Suggested Reading:
Weatherman, ed. by Harold Jacobs, Ramparts Press, c. 1970.

Robert Brustein, *Revolution as Theatre: Notes On the New Radical Style*, New York, Liveright, c. 1971.

David Dellinger, *Revolutionary Nonviolence*, New York, Bobbs-Merrill, c. 1970.

Alan Adelson, *SDS: A Profile*, New York, Scribner's, c. 1972.

Chapter 8—Igor Stravinsky

1. Marion Bauer & Ethel Peyser, *Music through the Ages*, ed. and rev. by Elizabeth E. Rogers, New York, Putnam's, c. 1932, p. 660.
2. Recorded in Paul Horgan's *Encounters with Stravinsky*, New York, Farrar, Strauss and Giroux, c. 1972, pp. 12-13.
3. S. L. Grigoriev, *The Diaghilev Ballet*, 1909-1929, London, Constable, 1953, Quoted in Eric Walter White's *Stravinsky: The Composer and His Works*, Los Angeles, UCLA Press, 1966, p. 27.
4. Bauer & Peyser, op. cit., p. 662.
5. Ibid.
6. Ibid.
7. *Stravinsky: A New Appraisal of His Work*, ed. by Paul Henry Lang, New York, Norton, c. 1963, p. 9.
8. White, op. cit., p. 28.
9. Horgan, op. cit., p. 13.
10. Edward T. Cone, "The Uses of Convention: Stravinsky and His Models," in Lang, op. cit., p. 21.
11. White, op. cit., p. 510.
12. Igor Stravinsky and Robert Craft, *Memories and Commentaries*, Garden City, New York, Doubleday, 1960. This incident is also discussed at some length in White, op. cit., pp. 95 ff.
13. This quote is attributed to Von Vechten by Horgan, op. cit., pp. 13-14.
14. Quoted by White, op. cit., p. 520.
15. Igor Stravinsky, *Poetics of Music in the Form of Six Lessons*, trans. by Arthur Knodel and Ingolf Dahl, Cambridge, Mass., Harvard University Press, 1947.
16. Igor Stravinsky and Robert Craft, *Expositions and Developments*, Garden City, New York, Doubleday, 1962.
17. White, op. cit., p. 523.

Chapter 9—James Joyce

1. Reported in L. A. G. Strong, *The Sacred River: An Approach to James Joyce*, New York, Pellegrini and Cudahy, c. 1951, p. 16.
2. James Joyce, *Ulysses*, New York, Random House, c. 1934 by Modern Library, new edition 1961. This selection is from an introductory letter of Joyce to Bennett Cerf, who was then the editor of Random House, p. xiii.
3. Mary and Padraic Colum, *Our Friend James Joyce*, New York, Doubleday, c. 1958, p. 12.
4. Quoted in Kevin Sullivan, *Joyce Among the Jesuits*, New York, Columbia University Press, 1954, p. 74. Some scholars maintain this story to be apocryphal.
5. David Daiches, *The Novel and the Modern World*, Chicago, University of Chicago Press, c. 1960, p. 85.
6. James Joyce, *A Portrait of the Artist as a Young Man*, New York, B. W. Huebsch, 1926, p. 518.
7. Richard Ellman, *James Joyce*, New York, Oxford University Press, 1959, p. 372.
8. Daiches, op. cit., pp. 99-100.
9. Judge John M. Woolsey, United States District Court of New York, *Opinion A. 110-59*, quoted in introduction to *Ulysses*, op. cit., pp. ix-x.
10. Adaline Glasheen, "Finnegans Wake and the Girls from Boston, Mass.," *Hudson Review*, Spring, 1954, p. xvi. Quoted by Herbert Howarth, *The Irish Writers: 1880-1940*, Hill and Wang, New York, 1958, p. 277.
11. Many thanks for this example to David Daiches, op. cit., p. 131.
12. Ibid.
13. Homer Obed Brown, *James Joyce's Early Fiction*, Cleveland, Case Western Reserve University Press, 1972, p. 9.
14. A. Walton Litz, *James Joyce*, New York, Twayne Publishers, c. 1966, pp. 99-100.
15. *Letters of James Joyce*, ed. by Stuart Gilbert, New York, Viking Press, 1957, pp. 274-275.
16. Herbert Howarth, *The Irish Writers: 1880-1940*, New York, Hill and Wang, 1958, p. 287.

Suggested Reading:
James Joyce, *A Shorter Finnegans Wake*, ed. by Anthony Burgess,

New York, The Viking Press, 1966.

Stanislaus Joyce, *My Brother's Keeper: James Joyce's Early Years*, ed. by Richard Ellman, New York, The Viking Press, c. 1958.

Richard K. Cross, *Flaubert and Joyce: The Rite of Fiction*, Princeton, New Jersey, Princeton University Press. 1971.

Chapter 10—Lenny Bruce

1. Kenneth Tynan in the Foreword to Lenny Bruce's *How to Talk Dirty and Influence People*, Chicago, Playboy Press, c. 1972, p. vi.
2. Albert Goldman, *Ladies and Gentlemen, Lenny Bruce!*, New York, Random House, 1974, p. 94. See also Bruce, op. cit., pp. 30-32.
3. Lenny Bruce, op. cit., pp. 234-235.
4. Goldman, op. cit., p. 166.
5. Ibid., p. 158.
6. Ibid., p. 164.
7. Ibid., pp. 393-394.
8. Ibid., pp. 394-395.
9. Ibid., p. 399.
10. Dick Schaap in the afterword to Bruce's *How to Talk Dirty and Influence People*, p. 237.

Suggested Reading:

Julian Barry, *Lenny*, New York, Grove Press, c. 1971.

Albert Goldman, "What Lenny Bruce Was All About," *The New York Times Biographical Edition*, June 27, 1971, pp. 2181-2185.

Chapter 11—The Fabulous Fowlers

1. *Stedman's Medical Dictionary*, 22nd edition, Baltimore, Williams and Wilkins Company, c. 1972, p. 968.
2. Arturo Castiglioni, M.D., *A History of Medicine*, trans. by E. B. Krumbhaar, M.D., Ph.D., New York, Alfred Knopf, c. 1941, p. 636. See also the notation in Gerhard Venzmer, *Five Thousand Years of Medicine*, trans. by Marion Koenig, New York, Taplinger Publishing Company, c. pp. 251-252.

3. As reported by Madeleine B. Stern, *Heads & Headlines: The Phrenological Fowlers*, Norman, Oklahoma, University of Oklahoma Press, c. 1971, p. xiv.

4. Ibid., p. xv.

5. Ibid., pp. 17-18.

6. Ibid., p. 18.

7. Clara Barton, *The Story of My Childhood*, New York, c. 1907, as reported by Stern, op. cit., p. 22.

8. Stern, op. cit., pp. 102-104.

9. Ibid., p. 105.

10. Orson Fowler, *Creative & Sexual Science*, p. 51, as taken from Stern, op. cit., pp. 193-195.

11. Stern, op. cit., p. 260.

12. Karl M. Dallenbach, "Phrenology versus Psychoanalysis," *The American Journal of Psychology*, 1955, vol. 68, p. 519.

Chapter 12—Sigmund Freud

1. Sigmund Freud, "History of the Psychoanalytic Movement," 1914. In *The Standard Edition of the Complete Psychological Works of Sigmund Freud*, ed. James Strachey. London, Hogarth Press, 1955 XIV, p. 44. *Standard Edition* references are hereafter abbreviated as *SE*.

2. Quoted in Ernest Cobones, *The Life and Work of Sigmund Freud*.

3. Ibid.

4. Ibid., p. 361.

5. Ibid., p. 403.

6. David Stafford-Clark, *What Freud Really Said*, New York, Schocken Books, c. 1966, p. 138.

7. Reuben Fine, *The Development of Freud's Thought*, New York, Aronson, Inc., c. 1973, p. 43.

8. *SE*, Vol. IV, p. xxxii.

9. Cobones, op. cit., II, p. 5.

10. Ibid., p. 6.

11. *SE*, Vol. XXIII, pp. 152-154.

12. Bernard G. Surant, *"Religion and the Extrapolation to Divinity,"* Insight: Quarterly Review of Religion and Mental Health, 1966, Vol. 4, p. 13. In this regard, see *Totem and Taboo, SE*, Vol. XIII, pp. 147-152.

13. Cobones, op. cit., Vol. II, p. 433.
14. Ibid.
15. Erich Fromm, *Sigmund Freud's Mission*, New York, Harper and Brothers, c. 1959, p. 2.
16. Ibid., p. 4.
17. Cobones, op. cit., Vol. II, p. 434.

Chapter 13—B. F. Skinner

1. This study was a doctoral dissertation by Rae Goodell entitiled "The Visible Scientists," as reported in *The APA Monitor*, Vol. 6 (8), August, 1975, pp. 8, 12.
2. B. F. Skinner, *Walden Two*, New York, Macmillan, 1948.
3. Skinner, *Science and Human Behavior*, New York, Macmillan, 1953, pp. 437-438.
4. Skinner, *Beyond Freedom and Dignity*, New York, Knopf, 1971, p. 5.
5. Ibid.
6. Ibid., pp. 19-21.
7. Walter Arnold, *The Saturday Review*, October 9, 1971, p. 48.
8. Peter Caws, "Psychology without a Psyche," *The New Republic*, October 16, 1971, p. 33.
9. Arnold, op. cit., p. 52.
10. George Kateb, "Toward a Wordless World," *The Atlantic Monthly*, October, 1971, p. 125.
11. W. F. Day, "Beyond Bondage and Regimentation," *Contemporary Psychology: A Journal of Reviews*, Vol. XVII, September, 1972, p. 467.
12. O. Hobart Mowrer, as quoted in *Contemporary Psychology*, Ibid., p. 470.
13. Finley Carpenter, *The Skinner Primer*, New York, The Free Press, 1974.
14. *Time*, September 20, 1971, p. 51.
15. Skinner, "Baby in a Box," *Ladies Home Journal*, October, 1945. Reprinted in Skinner, *Cumulative Record*, New York, Appleton-Century-Crofts, c. 1959, p. 573.
16. Ibid.
17. Skinner, *American Psychologist*, 1956, Vol. II, pp. 221-233. Reprinted in *Cumulative Record*, p. 101.

18. Ibid., p. 112.
19. Skinner, "Pigeons in a Pelican," *American Psychologist*, January, 1960. Reprinted in *Cumulative Record*, p. 585.
20. Ibid., p. 590.

Chapter 14—Toward a Theory of Individuality

1. David L. Miller, *Individualism: Personal Achievement and the Open Society*, Austin, University of Texas Press, c. 1967, p. 3.
2. Ibid.
3. Carol Hanisch, "The Personal Is Political," in Shulamith Firestone and Anne Koedt, eds., *Notes From the Second Year: Major Writings of the Radical Feminists*, New York, 1970, pp. 76-78.
4. Marshall Berman, *The Politics of Authenticity: Radical Individualism and the Emergence of Modern Society*, New York, Atheneum, 1970, p. xix.
5. From June K. Singer, *The Unholy Bible: A Psychological Interpretation of William Blake*, New York, Harper Colophon Books, 1970, p. 83.
6. From Robert Boyers and Robert Orrill, eds., *R. D. Laing and Anti-Psychiatry*, New York, Harper & Row, 1971, pp. 263-264.
7. Ken Kesey, *Sometimes A Great Notion*, New York, The Viking Press, 1964, pp. 71-72.

Index